FIELD GUIDE: HOW TO BE A
FASHION DESIGNER

ROCKPORT

FIELD GUIDE: HOW TO BE A
FASHION DESIGNER

Marcarena San Martin

BEVERLY MASSACHUSETTS

ROCKPORT PUBLISHERS

Copyright © 2009 by **maomao** publications
First published in 2009 in the United States of America by
Rockport Publishers, a member of
Quayside Publishing Group
100 Cummings Center
Suite 406-L
Beverly, MA 01915-6101
Telephone: (978) 282-9590
Fax: (978) 283-2742
www.rockpub.com

ISBN-13: 978-1-59253-491-3
ISBN-10: 1-59253-491-0

10 9 8 7 6 5 4 3 2 1

Publisher: Paco Asensio
Editorial coordination: Anja Llorella Oriol
Text edition: Macarena San Martín
Art director: Emma Termes Parera
Layout: Esperanza Escudero Pino, Raquel Marín Álvarez
English translation: Kevin Krell

Editorial project:
maomao publications
Via Laietana, 32, 4th fl, of. 92
08003 Barcelona, Spain
Tel.: +34 93 268 80 88
Fax: +34 93 317 42 08
www.maomaopublications.com

Printed in Singapore

CONTENTS

PREFACE

Many people dream of having their own fashion collection. And creating one may seem simple, with a good idea being all that is needed for the collection to be a success. However, in order for this happen, a series of elements and details need to be taken into consideration.

The first step is developing the designs, giving expression on paper to the ideas in one's head that will later be transformed into prototypes. While this can be done intuitively, certain tools facilitate the process, helping to carry it out in a methodical way and to obtain more effective results.

Once the collection has been properly developed, it is important to be absolutely clear about the audience it is intended for and the best place for selling it. Afterwards, one needs to determine the strategy for situating the collection at this point of sale, how it will be presented, and what means of communication or campaign will be used for advertising. All of these factors can alter the destiny of a collection.

The pages in this book offer a detailed sample of the path to success, as well as introducing the cast of characters that play a part in this trajectory, with whose help the process is less burdensome and more fruitful.

THE WORLD
OF FASHION

THE WORLD OF FASHION

WHAT IS FASHION?

While everybody talks about fashion nowadays, hardly anyone ever stops to consider what fashion truly is, what its origins are, or how it came to occupy all spheres of society. In our consumerist culture, nothing escapes its influence, and it is therefore safe to say that today fashion has become a way of life.

Conceived in the context of dress, fashion as a logic based on novelty has extended to all areas of society, a fact first confirmed in 1890, when the French sociologist Gabriel de Tarde defined it as a social process independent of dress. *Homo sapiens* are the only animals that wear clothes, and fashion came into being because men and women are social animals who, while desiring to belong to a group, also want to be different, as pointed out by the German sociologist Georg Simmel. Defining fashion is not easy, because fashion is multifaceted. It forms part of the culture and thus can be studied from multiple angles from the perspective of history, sociology, anthropology, psychology, art, economics, or science. Fashion is a complex process that reflects society's transformations in each age.

A scientific definition of fashion explains it as a social phenomenon that generates and is generated by constant and periodic variations in dress. This definition distinguishes fashion as a system based on constant change, that is, on newness.

REASONS AND PURPOSES OF DRESS

In 1930, the English psychologist John-Carl Flügel elucidated the primary causes, now universally accepted, as to why human beings wear clothes: modesty, protection, and adornment.

While modesty is a question of habit and convention (Judeo-Christian society demonizes nudity) and protection is situational (since it depends on the climate), adornment is the dominant motive of dress, given its presence in all cultures and at all times, regardless of the particular religion.

There are also three primary purposes of dress: to make visible the social distinction of a person, to express one's taste and personality, and to seduce, that is, to fit into a social group. The priority of these functions has changed over the course of history as a consequence of the evolution of society. Until the French Revolution, dress explicitly defined the social position of an individual, with very little room left for expressing one's personal style, while beginning in the twentieth century, and especially since the 1960s, the affirmation of individual identity has become the most important function of dress. Seduction has always been present, as it reflects the need to connect with a determined social group.

ORIGIN AND EVOLUTION OF FASHION

Fashion is a particular system of production and organization of dress that emerged in the West with the advent of modernity during the fourteenth century, subsequently expanding with the rise of mercantile capitalism, hand-in-hand with technological processes. Pre-modern societies were traditional —based on worship of the past, of tradition—perpetuating the same forms of dress with negligible alterations.

The system of fashion took root when a rupture from the past (from the old) in benefit of the future (the new) occurred. Which is to say, when newness became a constant and general principle, highlighting a predilection typical of the West: modernity.

The evolution of the fashion system can be divided into three stages:
- Aristocratic fashion appeared in the second half of the fourteenth century and lasted until the middle of the nineteenth century. Its dominant figure was masculine, with men exhibiting the full range of their power through a fashion based on ornamentation.
- Centennial fashion emerged in the second half of the nineteenth century and extended up to the 1960s. Men were eclipsed by women, who drew attention to themselves with haute couture designs.
- Open fashion was born in the '60s and continues to this day, characterized by the great interest of both sexes in their appearance, coinciding with the rise of consumer society.

ARISTOCRATIC FASHION

In Western society, up until the appearance of fashion, both sexes exhibited a similar figure, dressing in more or less long tunics that were tight-fitting at the waist.

In the mid-fourteenth century, attire became differentiated by gender: short and tight for men, long and enveloping for women. From its birth, fashion has indicated the position of both sexes in society. Men began wearing hose (bifurcated garments—the ancestors of pants—which were more suitable for male activities), highlighting the entire body, a reflection of their dominant sexual role. Meanwhile, women exhibited their classic curves—waist, breasts, hips—and concealed their legs beneath long skirts, thus declaring their role as the submissive sex. The emergence of fashion was marked by certain political, economic, social, and cultural factors. After the barbarian invasions, the West experienced a period of political stability that allowed for great economic expansion, accompanied by the growth of cities. Economic development and urban life facilitated the birth of a new social class, the mercantile and financial bourgeoisie, which would acquire its wealth from working, in contrast to the idle dominant aristocracy. According to the theory of historical materialism, to which most of the scholars who have written about fashion subscribe—from Thorstein Veblen to Pierre Bourdieu—the appearance of fashion reflected the latent tension that existed between the social classes. In the pyramidal society of the time, the bourgeoisie began to imitate the nobility, while the elite, in order to maintain social dis-

tance, found itself obliged to change its appearance to distinguish itself from its imitator. To make things easier, throughout Europe laws began to be passed, called sumptuary laws, that codified the dress of each class, reserving the distinction of luxury for the aristocratic classes. From this double movement of imitation and distinction emerged the mutability of fashion. A periodic and constant movement that would only accelerate over the centuries.

The French philosopher and sociologist Gilles Lipovetsky attests that the appearance of fashion also represented the beginning of the end of the power of the aristocracy. In order to continue occupying a place of prestige, this class was obliged to transform itself into a spectacular class, whose primary obligation was the ostentatious display of waste. In this sense, the nobles of the court competed for attention, as much through image as though the refinement of customs. The cultural factors that influenced the birth of fashion were the values of gentlemanly culture. Until then, men won women's love thanks to the virtues of virility. As a result of this new culture, a woman's love was now obtained through gallantry, thus initiating a process of seduction based on appearance and language.

During the second half of the Middle Ages, new social valuations emerged. The concept of the individual assumed another dimension, declaring the affirmation of a distinct personality among the dominant classes, which would later culminate in the *uomo singolare* of the Renaissance, to which was added the hedonism typical of aristocratic mores of the period.

CENTENNIAL FASHION

Throughout the second half of the nineteenth century, a system of production and communication of women's fashion—haute couture—appeared, unheard of until then. With the advent of the democratic era, ushered in by the French Revolution, bourgeois men renounced fashion, standardizing their dress in the form of the masculine suit—dark, austere, discreet—reminiscent of Protestantism, in order to clearly differentiate themselves from the toppled aristocracy. From then on women, by means of haute couture, became the showcase of masculine power, transformed into the bearers of the symbols of luxury and seduction. In this way haute couture came to be, in the democratic world, a mechanism of social distinction, destined to continue generating differences among the classes.

The father of haute couture was the Englishman Charles Frederick Worth, who in 1858 changed the rules of the game. Until then, tailors and dressmakers, in large part anonymous, worked at the service of clients, who provided them with ideas, materials, and adornments. Worth set forth his own creations, produced beforehand with fabric of his own choice. Moreover, this new way of thinking about fashion was accompanied by a new way of communicating fashion: Worth was the first to put a label bearing his name on dresses, thus creating brand image, and he presented his collections using young women out of which the modern fashion show would emerge.

OPEN FASHION

Consumer society, born in the wake of World War II due to technological advance and the increased availability of labor, expanded the desire for fashion to all social classes. This coincided with the consolidation and development of prêt-à-porter, or "ready to wear," which would definitively democratize fashion.

Consumer culture, oriented toward the present and the new, gave rise to a fresh phenomenon: the cult of youth. The new principal of social imitation was—and continues to be—young, which, in turn, gave rise to the cult of the body, ushering in fashion of a less formal style (sportswear, casualwear, streetwear). Furthermore, in the 1960s, young people vindicated new ways of being and appearing, symbolizing the first crisis of masculine identity, as men acquired a renewed taste for fashion. Since then, fashion no longer has had a single reference, the dominant class, but has entered the supermarket of styles where each person invents their own image, their own look, in a playful act of renewal. In a society as individual and hedonistic as ours, fashion answers increasingly less to class significations and more and more to signs of seduction, as it represents not merely a way of dressing but also, and more important, a set of values, that is, a way of life.

F.C.

THE TWENTIETH CENTURY IN 80 DESIGNERS

1. Alber Elbaz (1961)
2. Alberta Ferretti (1950)
3. Alexander McQueen (1969)
4. André Courrèges (1923)
5. Ann Demeulemeester (1954)
6. Azzendine Alaïa (1940)
7. Calvin Klein (1942)
8. Claire McCardell (1905–1958)
9. Claude Montana (1949)
10. Cristóbal Balenciaga (1895–1972)
11. Charles James (1906–1978)
12. Christian Dior (1905–1957)
13. Christian Lacroix (1951)
14. Christopher Bailey (1971)
15. Dolce & Gabbana (1959 & 1963)
16. Donna Karan (1948)
17. Dries van Noten (1958)
18. Elsa Schiaparelli (1890–1973)
19. Emilio Pucci (1914–1992)
20. Emmanuel Ungaro (1933)
21. Franco Moschino (1950–1994)
22. Frida Giannini (1972)
23. Gabrielle Chanel (1883–1971)
24. Gianfranco Ferré (1944–2007)
25. Gianni Versace (1946–1997)
26. Giorgio Armani (1934)
27. Grès (1903–1993)

28. Guy Laroche (1921–1989)
29. Hedi Slimane (1968)
30. Helmut Lang (1956)
31. Hubert de Givenchy (1927)
32. Issey Miyake (1938)
33. Jacques Doucet (1853–1929)
34. Jacques Fath (1912–1954)
35. Jacques Heim (1899–1967)
36. Jean Patou (1880–1936)
37. Jean-Louis Scherrer (1935)
38. Jeanne Lanvin (1867–1946)
39. Jean Paul Gaultier (1952)
40. Jil Sander (1943)
41. John Galliano (1960)
42. Karl Lagerfeld (1933)
43. Kenzo Takada (1939)
44. Louis Féraud (1920–1999)
45. Lucien Lelong (1889–1958)
46. Lucile (1863–1935)
47. Madeleine Vionnet (1876–1975)
48. Marc Jacobs (1963)
49. Marcel Rochas (1902–1955)
50. Mariano Fortuny (1871–1949)
51. Martin Margiela (1957)
52. Mary Quant (1934)
53. Michael Kors (1959)
54. Miuccia Prada (1949)

55. Narciso Rodríguez (1961)
56. Nicolas Ghesquière (1972)
57. Nina Ricci (1883–1970)
58. Nino Cerruti (1930)
59. Oliver Theyskens (1977)
60. Paco Rabanne (1934)
61. Paul Poiret (1879–1944)
62. Paul Smith (1946)
63. Pierre Balmain (1914–1982)
64. Pierre Cardin (1922)
65. Raf Simons (1968)
66. Ralph Lauren (1939)
67. Rei Kawakubo (1942)
68. Roberto Cavalli (1940)
69. Roy Halston (1932–1990)
70. Rudi Gernreich (1922–1985)
71. Sonia Rykiel (1930)
72. Stefano Pilati (1965)
73. Stella McCarney (1971)
74. Thierry Mugler (1948)
75. Tom Ford (1961)
76. Valentino Garavani (1932)
77. Viktor&Rolf (1969&1969)
78. Vivienne Westwood (1941)
79. Yohji Yamamoto (1943)
80. Yves Saint Laurent (1936–2008)

ORGANIZATION OF THE CURRENT FASHION SYSTEM

Ever since Barthélémy Thimmonier invented the sewing machine in 1830 (replacing artisanal labor with the mechanized production of dresses and thereby lowering costs), the fashion industry has undergone tremendous changes. Previously, buying a suit or dress was a complicated affair: one had to choose the fabric, accessories and adornments needed for making the garment; decide on the style; summon the tailor or dressmaker; wait several weeks and then endure more than one trial. The most complicated part about it, however, was knowing what one wanted in time. Some fabric merchants were aware of the advantage of producing designs beforehand, with the aim of exhibiting them as samples. This made the selection process easier for clients, who ended up buying the already finished product. For this reason, one of the most significant commercial innovations of the nineteenth century was the selling of previously made clothes: professional uniforms, men's suits, and garments for special occasions (mourning and wedding attire, coats) were made with cheap fabrics and in very basic styles. This kind of clothing was sold in large department stores and directed at the working class.

In the 1920s, another fashion factor—novelty—was introduced into the production of clothes when in the United States large department stores began to offer simplifications of haute couture designs from Paris, thus foreshadowing what would become prêt-à-porter.

Today, fashion is a motor that functions at different speeds. From haute couture to sportswear, from prêt-à-porter to casual to mass distribution, fashion production depends on different concepts and calendars conceived for the satisfaction of all sorts of people, given that fashion, nowadays is accessible to almost everyone.

HAUTE COUTURE
What is haute couture?

Haute couture is a system of fashion production and communication, born in the second half of the nineteenth century, whose main objective is to dress women in custom-made clothes. Today, the concept has changed, and despite the fact that haute couture is not a profitable activity, it represents nonetheless a major publicity campaign for brands that can afford it.

In 1858, Worth opened a Maison Spéciale de Confections in Paris, at 7, rue de la Paix, paving the way for haute couture, a system linked to the figure of the couturier, who, almost artisanally, dresses women in custom-made clothes. In 1869, the Chambre Syndicale de la Haute Couture was created, an entity which in 1911 defined the designation "house of fashion" as a business whose activity consisted in creating feminine designs for selling both to private clients and professionals.

The criteria for bestowing upon a company the denomination "house of haute couture"—an exclusively Parisian title—were elaborated in 1945.

Among the requirements were creating original designs by a permanent designer, producing custom-made designs, executing certain tasks by hand (basting, embroidery), having a studio in Paris with a minimum of employees (currently fifteen full-time workers), and showing a certain number of designs regularly in Paris. Over the years, the sector has been in decline. After World War II there were 106 houses of haute couture; in 2007 there were only ten. In 2001, the criteria were relaxed in order to avoid a complete collapse. This was not the first measure taken to rescue houses of haute couture. In 1997, with the same objective in mind, members were divided into three categories:

- full members
- correspondents, foreign members with the obligation of showing in Paris
- guests, aspirants sponsored by a member of the above two categories whose collections do not meet all the required criteria and who will only be bumped up to a superior category if they show regularly during certain seasons

Today, the qualification of haute couture is legally protected and can only be used by companies that appear in the list of one of the categories, established each year by a commission of the French Ministry for Industry.

CURRENT MEMBERS OF HAUTE COUTURE

MEMBERS OF HAUTE COUTURE	CORRESPONDENT MEMBERS	GUEST MEMBERS
Adeline André	Elie Saab	Adam Jones
Anne Valérie Hash	Armani Privé	Alexis Mabille
Chanel	Maison Martin Margiela	Atelier Gustavo Lins
Christian Dior	Valentino	Boudicca
Christian Lacroix		Cathy Pill
Dominique Sirop		Christophe Josse
Emanuel Ungaro		Felipe Oliveira Baptista
Franck Sorbier		Jean-Paul Knott
Givenchy		Josep Font
Jean Paul Gaultier		Lefranc Ferrant
Maurizio Galante		Marc Le Bihan
		Richard René
		Stéphane Rolland
		Udo Edling
		Wuyong

Haute couture clients

Clients interested in buying haute couture have traditionally been:

- Private clients: wealthy women that form part of international high society for whom the selected design is custom-made, which implies several trials. Over the years, this type of client has decreased from around 20,000 before World War II to less than 200 today. It is important to keep in mind that some dresses can end up costing more than 100,000 euros ($136,000).
- Professional buyers: in the early days of haute couture they were primarily buyers from large American department stores, which could purchase original designs—by sizes, and at a 40 percent mark up compared to private clients—with the right to reproduce them industrially or buy test garments and patterns directly, which, in addition to being able to be reproduced industrially, were adapted to the store's own production models. In some cases, and under very restrictive conditions, big department stores could associate their names with the creator of haute couture on labels. This type of buying suffered a major blow in 1929, as a consequence of the New York stock market crash, and would stop in the 1980s with the rise of designer prêt-à-porter. This was due to the fact that it was now unnecessary to pay such exorbitant amounts for garments that became luxury prêt-à-porter the moment they left Paris.

While haute couture represents a part of women's fashion with an increasingly diminished clientele, men's tailoring continues to represent a

© Raul Benegas. Design: Dominique Sirop. Haute couture SS 2009

mode of creating extremely signifi-cant fashion. Also known as tailoring, this process of fashioning men's suits involves customized production, as in the case of haute couture, although today it exists alongside the industrial methods of large distribution chains.

Fashion shows

Haute couture collections are exhib-ited by way of fashion shows. Initially, each house organized its own show independently until the 1930s when a common calendar was established. Currently, the entity that regulates fashion shows is the Fédération Fran-çaise de la Couture, du Prêt-à-porter des Couturiers et des Créateurs de Mode (www.modeaparis.com), which was created in 1973. Haute couture shows are held in Paris twice a year, always before prêt-à-porter shows, in January for the spring-summer season and in July for the fall-winter season.

PRÊT-À-PORTER
What is prêt-à-porter?

Prêt-à-porter is serialized production with the added value of the concept of fashion, that is, of change with each new season. Emerging during World War II in the United States, under the name "ready to wear," it gained strength in the 1960s in tandem with the figure of the fashion designer, who planned collections for industrial pro-duction, and the boutique, a new way of selling clothes.

As far back as the 1920s, large Ameri-can department stores had already introduced the fashion factor into

(continued on p.30)

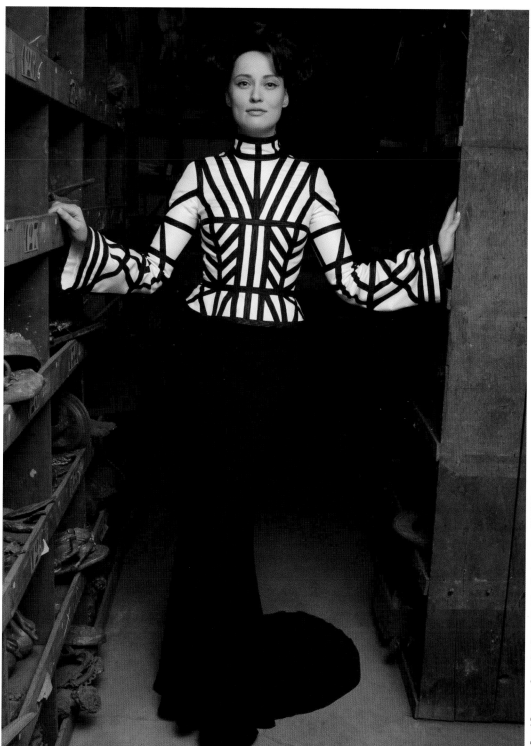

© Olivia Hemus. Design: CYBÉLE

their production departments, aimed at the general public with simplifications inspired by haute couture. World War II isolated Paris, and the United States was forced to create its own style. The American look was inspired by designer Claire McCardell, who created her collections based on the concept of combinable garments to be serially reproduced for the general public, thus giving rise to "ready to wear." In 1949, the French translation prêt-à-porter appeared, and Robert Weill and Albert Lempereur, the two most important French clothes manufacturers of the period, created their own brands, associating them with the term *prêt-à-porter*.

Along with this new method of creating industrialized fashion, a new way of buying clothes was born. The boutique, or fashion shop, first appeared in London with Mary Quant's Bazaar (1955) and John Stephen's His Clothes (1958), a phenomenon that grew in the 1960s with the triumph of youth fashion. Within these shops, a new protocol for selling emerged, one that remains in place today: background music, the importance of shop windows, salespeople wearing the same clothes they are selling, dressing rooms, immediate accessibility to articles, etc.

Youth fashion became a business thanks to prêt-à-porter, and it was at this time that the figure of the fashion designer came into prominence, the specialist who conceives garments for serial production and works for a ready-to-wear brand. Starting in 1970, the concept of the "fashion creator" appeared, as designers began to emerge from anonymity, creating brands bearing their names and personal styles. As a result, street fashion stepped up onto fashion runways and shows became media spectacles.

Styles within prêt-à-porter

Prêt-à-porter includes two of the most popular styles on the street today: casualwear and streetwear.

Casual is a style that borrows certain elements from sportswear, placing emphasis on comfort and personal expression. It emerged in the United Kingdom in the late 1970s, within the sphere of soccer, when the non-violent working-class fans of Liverpool decided to adopt a definitive aesthetic—one that would differentiate them from violent skins and punks—based on the veneration of certain brands that originated on the continent. These fans followed their teams across Europe, where they had the opportunity to discover new brands that did not exist in the United Kingdom (Lacoste, Fila, Ellesse, Sergio Tacchini, Kappa, Stone Island, Slazenger, Diadora, Adidas, and Puma).

LIMITED EDITION
LEVI'S 1947
501 JEANS

Levi's Antwerp store, 501 room

This enabled them to create an identity distinct from the fans of other teams, reaffirming their loyalty through a hitherto unknown aesthetic.

Streetwear is a style characterized by a youthful, urban aesthetic based on simple garments, especially ones made of cotton, among which T-shirts, denim, and athletic shoes stand out.

SPORTSWEAR
History of sportswear

Sportswear was a response to a need for convenience and comfort when dressing to play sports, and its pre-history dates back to late eighteenth century in the United Kingdom, when the British style of dress stood in opposition to the French.

The male English aristocrat, a property owner, spent much of his time on his land, overseeing his property and practicing such sports as horseback riding and hunting. His clothes—necessarily practical—were discreet, comfortable, and resistant, and thus very different from the attire of the French court, which was delicate and loaded with embroidery. Ever since, Anglomania has been a constant in men's fashion, having become the model of modern elegance due to its comfort with a certain informality. The English-style suit was first for sport, then for travel, and, finally, for the city.

Design: Lacoste. SS 2009 at New York Fashion Week

Design: Lacoste. SS 2008, 75th anniversary collection at New York Fashion Week

The variety of sports activities, life in the open air, and travel by the upper classes beginning at the end of the nineteenth century necessitated a renewal of the wardrobes of both sexes, as these new activities demanded new attire based on convenience and comfort. In the 1920s, sportswear marked men's fashion with a soft and comfortable wardrobe in which knit garments were triumphant. Women began practicing sports en masse, as fashion now demanded a slim figure, and creators such as Coco Chanel, with her collections of knits, and Jean Patou paved the way for feminine sportswear. After World War II, sportswear began to triumph in Europe. Clothes for leisure time became more informal, especially beginning in the 1970s when, as a consequence of the need to be in shape and practice sports, the soft wardrobe of sportswear—sweatshirts, leotards, bodysuits, T-shirts, legwarmers, tops, tracksuits, and training shoes—began to be worn on the street. Fashion entered sports brands fully in the 1980s, when labels became aware of the added value represented by these garments, which until then had been more or less standard.

With sports fully integrated into society as a form of leisure, from the late twentieth century on, sports brands have entered the world of fashion with increasing frequency, utilizing prêt-à-porter designers as a lure to sell their collections. Ever since French tennis player René Lacoste, following his retirement in 1933, entered into a partnership with André Gillier, owner of the biggest knit factory in France, to create sports shirts with a crocodile logo, the relationship between sport and fashion has only grown stronger. Lacoste, nicknamed "the crocodile," broke with the rules of tennis by abandoning the traditional long-sleeve cotton shirt for a short-sleeve V-neck design, made of light, transpirable material (pique cotton) and inspired by the shirt worn to play polo, far more suitable for the movements of tennis.

Puma, defined today as a sportlifestyle company, was the first to unite fashion with sports, beginning a collaboration with the German designer Jil Sander in 1998. Later, Neil Barret (1999), Philip Stark (2004), Yasuhiro Mihara (2005), and Alexander McQueen (2006) appeared on the scene. Recently purchased by the luxury holding company PPR, Puma hired Hussein Chalayan as its artistic director with the objective of positioning the label as a trendsetting brand. Yet it was Adidas that scored the first media goal when it hired Japanese designer Yohji Yamamoto to launch its exclusive 2002 sportswear line "Y-3," ("Y" for Yamamoto, "3" for the emblematic stripes of the German brand), a collection inspired by sports but not intended for playing sports, making Adidas the first luxury "sport-à-porter" brand.

The sportswear trilogy

The most universal sportswear trilogy—T-shirt, tracksuit and sneakers—has origins dating back to the nineteenth century. The cotton T-shirt, which appeared with the development of underwear, was, at first, a men's garment used as much for staying warm as for sport. The name "T-shirt" indicates both its form and one of its most common uses: training (shirt).

The tracksuit was originally a thick, ribbed sweater worn by vegetable vendors in the Parisian market Les Halles. Initially, it was called "game-sou," a union of the word "Gamard" (the Amiens manufacturer that sold them) and the phonetics of the word "sweater" (garment for sweating). It ended up being called "chandail," (sweater) in 1894, becoming the prototype of the modern sweatshirt.

Sneakers appeared around 1860, when rubber soles were united to the upper part of canvas lace-up shoes thanks to the discovery of the vulcanization of rubber by Charles Goodyear. In 1895, English athlete Joseph William Foster came up with the design for a sneaker with a spiked sole, the Spike of Fire, which he went on to produce. Due to the success of this shoe, top athletes began to order Fosters, a brand that functioned successfully until 1958, when two of the grandchildren of the founder—Joseph and Jeffrey Foster—separated from the company and founded Reebok. In 1917, Converse All-Stars appeared—high-top athletic shoes that for many years were the most popular footwear for playing basketball in the United States.

In 1920, brothers Adolf and Rudolf Dassler began producing athletic shoes, but it was not until 1948 that

© Puma. *Running* collection

they founded Adidas. That year, due to a familial dispute, Rudolf left the company and founded Puma, provoking fierce competition.

During the 1950s, athletic shoes were adopted as a distinguishing feature by teenagers, as they were affordable and easy to obtain. James Dean made them a symbol of rebellion, in the movie *Rebel Without a Cause*.

In 1964, Phil Knight, a young university athlete, and Bill Bowerman, the legendary track–and–field coach at the University of Oregon and of the U.S. Olympic team, created BRS (Blue Ribbon Sports), a company devoted to selling Japanese running shoes, which were comfortable, light, and cheap. Given their success, they began designing the shoes themselves and then sending them to Japan to be made. Thus, in 1971, Nike was born.

In the 1980s, athletic shoes began to appear outside of their original context and on the street, a fashion that soon caught on like wildfire. The influence of casual British style—increasingly international—and the rise of hip-hop—the aesthetic of which was based primarily on the look of the artists' sports heroes— contributed decisively to the success of brand sportswear, ultimately becoming a uniform of status. On the other hand, the New York transportation strike in the spring of 1980, which lasted for eleven days, forced men and women to walk to work in

their sneakers, which proved that athletic shoes made for excellent urban footwear. Another important factor dates back to 1982, when the aerobics craze impelled Reebok to come out with the Reebok Freestyle, the first athletic shoe designed specifically for the female foot.

In the 1990s, so-called risk sports, which pay special attention to footwear, gained popularity among young people. One of the clearest examples was skateboarding, which appeared in California in the early 1960s as an offshoot of surfing and has subsequently become an urban subculture unto itself, with its own styles of dress.

LARGE-SCALE DISTRIBUTION

For some decades now, multinational fashion distribution companies have been growing not only in size but also in economic and social influence, being one of the greatest promoters and exponents of the process of globalization.

Their growth strategy is based on five points:
- Own market penetration
- Internationalization
- Vertical integration
- Diversification
- Affordable prices

On a global scale, the three most important large distribution chains are, in this order, Gap, the Spanish Inditex, and the Swedish H&M. Unique among them is Inditex, group owner of Zara, among other brands, which differentiates itself from the competition by vertically integrating the entire process involved in creating a garment (design, production, distribution, and management of stores); Gap and H&M design and sell but do not manufacture their clothes. This way of doing things has changed the rules of the game of fashion production and distribution.

Gap

In 1969, Don and Doris Fisher opened the first Gap store in San Francisco, with the idea of creating a brand that offered basic and simple garments such as T-shirts and blue jeans. Since then, Gap Inc., owner of the Gap, Banana Republic, Old Navy, and Piperlime brands, has become one of the most important large distribution chains, with 3,100 stores spread across the world.

Inditex

Currently Grupo Inditex (Industry and Textile Design) owns the following brands: Zara, Massimo Dutti, Pull&Bear, Bershka, Stradivarius, Oysho, Zara Home, Uterqüe, and Kiddy's Class. This successful group was born in 1985 in Arteixo (A Coruña, Spain), the result of the initiative of Amancio Ortega, an intuitive self-taught man who, after having worked as a salesclerk in a clothing store, founded, in 1963, GOA Confecciones, a company dedicated to the production of women's lingerie. In 1975, he decided to become a distributor and vendor as well, opening the first Zara store in A Coruña, a business model that has revolutionized, both economically and socially, the worlds of production and fashion. Today Zara accounts for 78 percent of the business of Inditex, with 1,425 stores in seventy countries in Europe, Asia, and America, situated in the most desirable commercial locations of major cities. Zara stores are elegant and modern, offering the most up-to-date fashion and good service at affordable prices. With new collections every two weeks, the Zara model has given rise to a climate of scarcity and opportunity, triggering continuous changes in fashion. Until its appearance, balance in the sector consisted of two seasons a year (spring-summer, fall-winter), which lasted for four months, followed by sales.

Zara's philosophy is based on the idea of the store as an information, image, and communication center, as its best advertising tool is its own shop windows, updated each month. But Zara stores are much more than their image: they are a vital information center. Once the business day ends, the store manager informs the head office, on a daily basis, what designs have sold—what sizes and colors—and which ones have enjoyed the most success so that repositionings can be planned. This information is passed on immediately to the creative department (consisting of some 200 designers). The patterns are then sent to the factory (a totally automated process), with the finished product ending up in the logistics center, which, twice a week, distributes new designs to all the stores. It takes about ten to fifteen days for new designs to arrive, from the initial drawing to its appearance in the store, while a con-

© Bershka

ventional designer spends six months on a design and another three on the production process before the product reaches the store.

Zara has a permanent collection, the basics, which represents 60 percent of its production, while the remaining 40 percent is known as "just-in-time" items, new garments that appear in the store every two weeks. With this system, 11,000 models are produced a year, and since production is a function of demand, there are no stocks, which allows for considerable savings in expenses.

H&M

In 1947, retailer Erling Persson, upon returning to his native city of Västerås (Sweden), decided to open a women's clothing store, which he named Hennes, or "For her." He had recently visited the United States, where large-volume clothing stores with affordable prices had made a strong impression on him. In 1968, wanting to establish himself in Stockholm, he bought Mauritz Widforss, a gunsmith's shop and hunting goods store. The purchase of the store included the men's clothing stock as well, and the business changed its name to Hennes&Mauritz.

With the slogan "Fashion and quality at the best price," H&M is present today in twenty-nine countries, with 1,500 stores, and produces 500 million articles a year, with daily repositionings. It does not have its own factories, allowing it to reduce costs and invest in advertising, in contrast to Inditex.

THE WORLD OF LUXURY

In opposition to the large distribution system—massive and offering affordable prices—there exists a totally different system of fashion, though one very typical of the design world: luxury. Traditionally, luxury has been defined as a way of life associated with wastefulness and ostentation, which is why for many years it was first limited to the aristocracy and later to the well-to-do classes. In the twentieth century, luxury became relative and plural, affordable to everyone according to their aspirations. In the new millennium, moreover, luxury has become emotional.

In order for a brand to be considered a luxury label, its products must satisfy certain requirements that revolve around material values (quality, price, artisanal savoir-faire) and immaterial values (heritage, the marked difference from the rest), though a certain distance with respect to the client is also necessary (exclusivity, difficulty of access). Luxury products tend to be centered around quality, but a quality product, a computer, for example, is not necessarily a luxury item. Likewise, the product of a luxury brand is not necessarily a quality item, for example, gadgets. Furthermore, luxury items are not the same thing as luxury brands; certain luxury items, such as caviar or truffles, make no reference to a brand.

Not all luxury brands are the same. Luxury identity is defined by the notion of a brand and cultural anchorage, which authenticates and legitimizes a brand, ostentation, and the status it confers, as well as resistance to the passage of time.

Evolution of luxury

The history of luxury can be divided into three periods, each with a different style:

- In the eighteenth century, and especially throughout the nineteenth century, a kind of luxury dominated by the beauty of the objects and the reputation of the house where they were acquired appeared in Europe. This was a classic luxury that needed to be visibly ostentatious. Example: Hermès.
- In the twentieth century, beginning in the 1920s, a concept of luxury in which the figure of the creator—from then on to be venerated for his capacity for innovation—appeared in Europe and the United States, in which the mere fact of novelty was a value in itself. Example: Chanel
- In the 1960s, a concept of luxury emerged in the United States endorsed by large-scale communication, in which what was important was not the object in itself but rather the global universe created by the media—contemporary luxury dominated by communication. Example: Ralph Lauren.

Today these three types of luxury coexist, feeding off one another.

The luxury market

This market consists of seven sectors:

- Perfume and cosmetics
- Fashion
- Alcoholic beverages
- Jewelry and watches
- Leather goods and shoes
- Fashion accessories
- Restoration

The global luxury market continues to grow due to the emergence of new markets such as those in China, India, and Russia; it is estimated that the luxury industry moves more than 10 billion euros ($14 billion) a year. Regarding products, the growth of accessories, shoes, leather goods, and jewelry has outstripped that of fashion and perfume.

With access to the licensing system since the 1950s—implemented in fashion thanks to Christian Dior—the strategy of luxury brands began to change, shifting from selling many

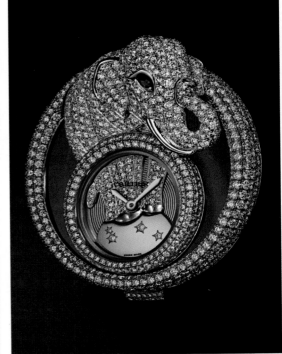

MAIN LUXURY HOLDING COMPANIES

LVMH (Louis Vuitton Moët Henessy)
Country: France
Founded: 1987
President: Bernard Arnault
Main brands: Louis Vuitton, Dior, DKNY, Berluti, Céline, Givenchy, Emilio Pucci, Kenzo, Loewe, Fendi, Marc Jacobs, Thomas Pink, Kenzo, StefanoBi, Guerlain, Chaumet, Fred Joailler, TAG Heuer, Hublot, Moët & Chandon, Veuve Clicquot, Krug, Sephora, Le Bon Marché, La Samaritaine, Acqua di Parma, Benefit Cosmetics, Make Up For Ever, Fresh, Labrosse et Dupont, eLuxury
Web: www.lvmh.fr

PPR (Printemps, Pinault, Redoute)
Country: France
Founded: 1963
President: François-Henri Pinault (son of founder François Pinault)
Main brands: Gucci Group (Gucci, Yves Saint Laurent, Bottega Veneta, Alexandre McQueen, Sergio Rossi, Boucheron, Stella McCartney, Bédat & Co, Balenciaga), La Redoute, Printemps, FNAC, Conforama, Puma, Château Latour, Christie's
Web: www.ppr.com

Richemont
Country: Switzerland
Founded: 1988
President: Johann Rupert
Main brands: Cartier, Van Cleefs & Arpels, Piaget, Baume et Mercier, Internacional Watch Co, Jaeger-LeCoultre, A. Lange & Söhne, Officine Panerai, Vacheron Constantin, Alfred Dunhill, Lancel, Montblanc, Montegrappa, Jamens Purdey & Sons, Chloé, Shangai Tang
Web: www.richemont.com

products to few customers to selling few products, though with a wide range, to many customers. In this way, luxury has moved from being an elite form of consumption to a "democratic" one.

In the 1990s there was a slight recession in the luxury market—a consequence of the Gulf War—and the industry began to reorganize itself into large groups (holdings), which adopted the notion of internationalization as one its main strategies.

GLOSSARY

American look: style created in the United States after World War II, based on the creation of collections made up of combinable garments, intended for mass reproduction for the general public.

Aristocratic fashion: fashion based on ornamentation, in which the male figure is dominant. It appears in the period beginning in the second half of the fourteenth century and lasting until the middle of the nineteenth century.

Barthélémy Thimmonier: inventor of the sewing machine (1830).

Boutique: small clothing store.

Casualwear: dress style that emphasizes comfort and personal expression.

Centennial fashion: fashion in which women are the centerpiece, featuring haute-couture designs. It appears in the second half of the nineteenth century and lasts until the 1960s.

Charles Frederick Worth: creator of haute couture.

Claire McCardell: designer who inspired the American look following World War II.

Couturier: clothes designer.

Denim: a fabric originally used in the production of work clothes, and today a sector unto itself within the fashion industry.

Fédération Française de la Couture, du Prêt-à-porter des Couturiers et des Créateurs de Mode: regulatory organization of haute-couture fashion shows.

Gamesou: original name for a tracksuit, the result of the combination of the word "Gamard" and the phonetics of sweater.

Haute couture: system of fashion production and communication that came into existence in the second half of the twentieth century, the main objective of which is to custom-dress women.

Just in time: new garments sent to stores every two weeks for repositioning of stock.

New York Stock Exchange Crash: the most devastating fall in the equities market in the history of the Stock Market, in October of 1929.

Open fashion: current fashion, in which both men and women demonstrate great interest in their appearance, coinciding with the rise of consumer society.

Prêt-à-porter: also called "ready to wear," mass production with the added value of "fashion."

"Ready to wear:" *see* Prêt-à-porter.

Savoir-faire: know-how, practical knowledge concerning a material.

Sportswear trilogy: T-shirt, tracksuit, and athletic shoes.

Streetwear: dress style characterized by a young urban aesthetic, based on elemental garments.

Sumptuary laws: laws that limit luxury and excessive expense. In the period of aristocratic fashion, they were applied in order to codify the manner of dressing of each social strata, reserving the distinction of luxury to the upper class.

Tailoring: making, repairing, or alteration of men's garments.

Uomo singolare: literally "singular man;" refers to the individual that constructs his character in the staging of different roles combined into one, characteristic of the Renaissance.

DEVELOPMENT PROCESS

DEVELOPMENT PROCESS

In order to develop a fashion collection one needs a great deal of creativity, a quality generally considered to be innate, and a gift that flowers on its own. Yet, the creative processes that lead to success are the result of the ability to come up with original solutions to concrete problems and situations that, beyond talent and individual gifts, stem from certain methodologies of work. As Pablo Picasso said, "Inspiration exists, but it has to find you working." Good ideas, important contributions, and new solutions are the consequences of specific procedures in which analysis, observation, reflection, and proposals form part of the same mechanism that encompasses distinct mental processes.

In the development of a fashion collection, then, proper planning is a must, and toward this end a series of steps should be followed.
- Look for references.
- Create a sketchbook.
- Define silhouettes, lines, colors, materials and fabrics.
- Produce a concept book or thematic panel.
- Develop patterns and test garments.
- Create prototypes.

REFERENCES

Prior to undertaking the creation of a clothing line or collection, the fashion designer must immerse himself in a process of investigation that permits finding and detecting inspirational sources, ones that potentially can be transformed into new products. It is not easy to guess what the public will want the next season—especially when one is working a year before it even begins. Thus, in order to be able to gather the resources needed for the proper planning of the collection, it is imperative to carry out a wide-ranging assessment of what is going on in the world. For this, one needs to be up-to-date regarding fashion, social, and consumer trends; know what is happening in the fashion industry and other sectors; and, above all, have personal interests that can be transformed into potential themes and ideas.

The result of a collection depends not only on the selection of a motif but also on how the motif is treated, developed, and applied to the garment. Maintaining all five senses alert—especially the visual sense—is one of the keys to creativity as the search for references for a collection

can emerge from diverse sources: books, magazines, movies, travels, icons, fictional characters, photographers, artists, inventions, architecture, music, places, tales, stories, plants, gastronomy, television, materials, the street, technology, websites, gadgets, blogs, etc. All the ideas culled during this search can be captured in a sketchbook.

THE SKETCHBOOK

The sketchbook is a notebook that reflects the creative process of the designer. It is a means of expression where ideas are collected and proposals are developed freely, with the aim of presenting the conceptual character of the collection, the making of the garments, the search for materials and fabrics, and the suggestions of possible looks. It functions as a travel book as well as a tool that allows one to explore the sources of inspiration for the collection personally and by hand.

The ideas developed in the sketchbook derive from two sources:
- Observation: centered primarily on external documentation that might include clippings from magazines, texts, advertising, photographs, small objects, etc.
- Invention: original ideas that are given expression on paper through text and/or drawings.

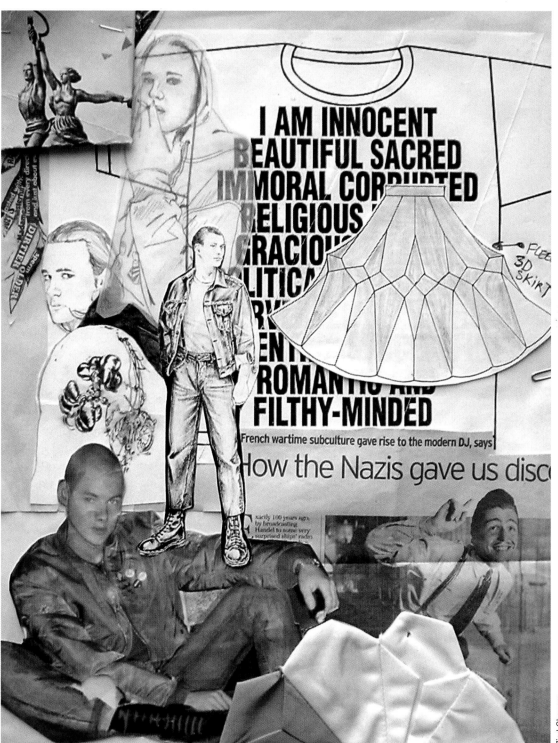

I AM INNOCENT
BEAUTIFUL SACRED
IMMORAL CORRUPTED
RELIGIOUS
GRACIOUS
LITICA
RV
ENT
ROMANTIC AND
FILTHY-MINDED

French wartime subculture gave rise to the modern DJ, says

How the Nazis gave us disc

FLEE
3D
SKIRT

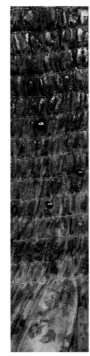

© Davina Hawthorne

© Davina Hawthorne

The formats, materials, applications, sizes, volumes, and textures are totally at the designer's discretion and will depend on what happens to be most comfortable for her in terms of expression, from the use of a simple notepad to a suitcase filled with references. The techniques, at the same time, are extremely varied, as they depend on the particular intention of the designer. The most commonly used method is collage, which allows for cutting, gluing, drawing, and assembly.

The ultimate objective of the sketchbook is to first obtain proposals which later will evolve and be transformed into a fashion collection.

To begin with, there are certain very important factors to keep in mind as they will help to specify, identify, and define ideas better. These elements are silhouettes, lines, colors, materials, and fabrics.

SILHOUETTES AND LINES

The twentieth century was a time of change as much in the social as the economic sphere, shifts that had an inevitable impact on fashion. Over the decades women came to take on a different role with their own dress and styles—the young, free-spirit of the 1920s or the "ideal" wife of the 1950s—becoming in the process an iconic fig-

ure that even today is still used as a reference for defining a collection.

The silhouette, being the first impression one has of a garment, dictates the general spirit of the collection from the get-go. For this reason, it will serve as a guide in the making of each of the garments and will determine, among other details, the volumes, the proportions, and materials—for example, a geometric silhouette will need a more rigid fabric than a free-flowing silhouette.

The standard term used for defining silhouettes is the line, articulated by the cut, the placement of pleats, and the effect these create. There are various kinds of lines: the A line, which refers to a garment that is narrow in the upper part with a low waist that widens toward the lower extreme; the trapezoid line, recognized by its broad backs and non-round forms that extend to the lower border of the garment; and the Y line, characterized by very wide shoulders with narrow skirts or straight pants, to name a few.

To preserve coherency and order in a collection, it is important to maintain common lines or details that recur throughout the pieces.

COLOR

Color is fundamental to the conception of a collection. It is one of the factors that first draws the attention of consumers, conveying the spirit and emotions that the collection wishes to express: sensuality, mystery, innocence, maturity, madness, etc. Such

is its importance that over the history of contemporary fashion, there have been designers associated with a particular color to the extent that it identifies them, resulting in a symbiosis where one cannot exist without the other, such as the case of Lanvin blue, Valentino red, or the shocking pink of Elsa Schiaparelli.

In order to create a color menu (a selection of between four and ten tones to be used in the production of a collection, some more frequently as base colors, others exclusively for details) it is important to keep in mind the three dimensions of a color if one wishes to obtain a chromatically harmonious color menu in which nothing is too shrill:

– Color: the color itself, such as red, blue or yellow.

– Value: the degree of luminosity or darkness a color has. The highest or most luminous values of a color are its hues and the lowest or darkest are its shadows.

– Saturation: the degree of intensity of a color, the brightness or paleness that it emits depending on its level of purity; when it is pure, and neither black nor white or any other color has been added to it, the color is at its maximum level of saturation.

Playing with colors and their dimensions in various ways produces different harmonic ranges:

– Monochromatic range: the selection of a single color; varying its saturation and/or value produces different shades.

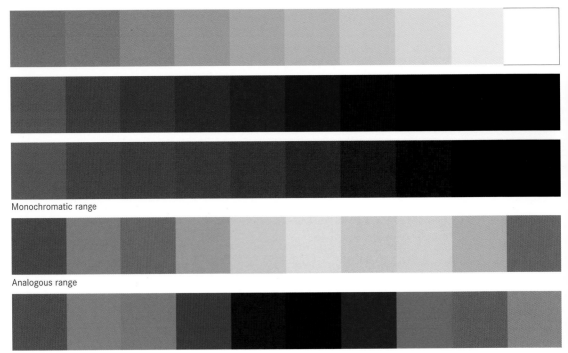

Monochromatic range

Analogous range

Complementary range

– Analogous range: the result of using two or three colors closely situated in the chromatic circle (analogous) and some of its shades, also the result of the variation of value and/or saturation.
– Complementary range: the result of the use of two complementary colors and their shades, obtained in the same way as in the above-mentioned cases.

MATERIALS AND FABRICS

It is essential to know the materials one is going to work with. The textures, the production processes, and the properties of a fiber or fabric are factors that can influence the final result of the garment, as much with regard to manufacturing and composition as price.

FIBERS

Fibers are divided into three blocks, according to their provenance:
– Natural: those that are made from animal components (wool, silk), vegetable (cotton, linen, canvas), and minerals (asbestos, Lurex).
– Artificial: those that come from natural elements but undergo an industrial transformation (above all, cellulose fibers like Lycocell and Nodal) and that possess properties similar to natural fibers.

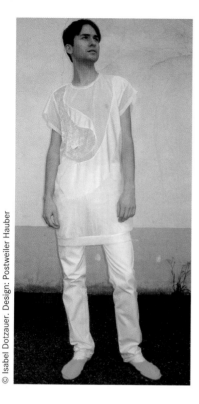

© Isabel Dotzauer. Design: Postweiler Hauber

© Ines Unser. Design: Postweiler Hauber

– Synthetic: these are produced entirely from chemical products that are relatively easy to find and for the most part inexpensive, such as coal, tar, ammonia, and petroleum, in addition to byproducts derived from industrial processes.

Fibers represent a highly dynamic and fascinating field. Nowadays much research is carried out in the search for new revolutionary fibers that contribute to increasing the value of garments. Among the most common lines of investigation is nanotechnology, which incorporates microcapsules replete with cosmetic properties that detach when they come in contact with the skin or electrical conductor wires with which it is possible to produce garments capable of charging a cellular phone or having points of light.

Other innovations are perhaps not as spectacular but nonetheless important. An example are new elastic fibers. These are much more resistant to highly abrasive chemical products, such as the ones used to give jeans a vintage look, and prevent wrinkles, making them ideal for shirts and suits. There are others that, despite being synthetic or artificial, involve an environment-friendly production process and are even biodegradable.

FABRICS

Fabrics are the cloths that result from the joining of threads, filaments, and fibers. Currently their presence in the market is so varied it is common to find different dictionaries in each country that enumerate and classify them. Specialized magazines are also a good tool for learning about innovations in this field, as new fiber discoveries lead to new fabrics. There are two primary methods of production for obtaining these materials. One is continuous fabric production (responsible for cloth and knit fabrics) and the other is discontinuous production, which is responsible for the manufacturing of felt, netting, lace, and glued fabrics, classified as nonfabrics:

– Fabric cloths: obtained by interweaving vertically arranged threads at right angles, the warp, which will form the long side of the cloth, with threads positioned horizontally, the weft. Depending on the density of the threads in the warp and the weft, and how these are combined, different fabrics are created.

– Knit fabric: obtained by knitting loops of thread, arranged either in the direction of the warp or the weft. The way in which the horizontal rows and the vertical rows are joined give this type of fabric its elasticity. Woven-knit fabric, formed by loops interwoven along the weft, has a construction similar to that of weaving, although more complicated, making it more resistant and less inclined to come apart.

– Nonfabrics: the result of the compression of fabrics through the application of heat, friction, or chemical products. These fabrics do not have longitudinal fibers, so they can be cut in any direction. They can be artificial, such as felt or latex, or natural, such as leather and fur.

It is important that fabrics respect the philosophy of the collection and that they be coherent with what has been designed; if they are medium-high or high-range garments, the fabric chosen must be in keeping with them.

ACCESSORIES

Buttons, ribbons, trimming, embroidery, crystal, studs, etc.—they are the details often applied to a basic conventional design, transforming it into another piece within the collection, one that stands out and makes a difference. As with other elements that must be studied and taken into consideration when planning a collection, it is fundamental to be precise in the selection of accessories and to maintain a certain degree of coherency.

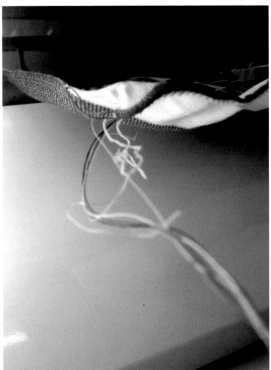

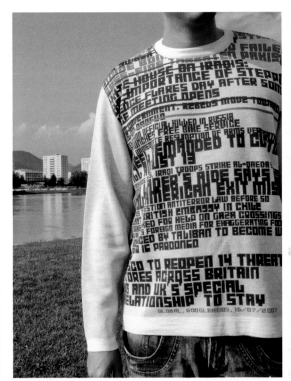

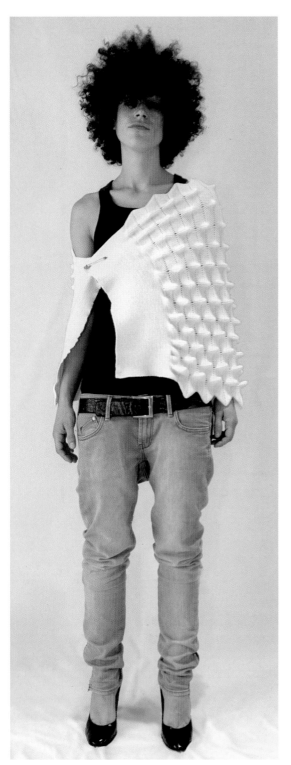
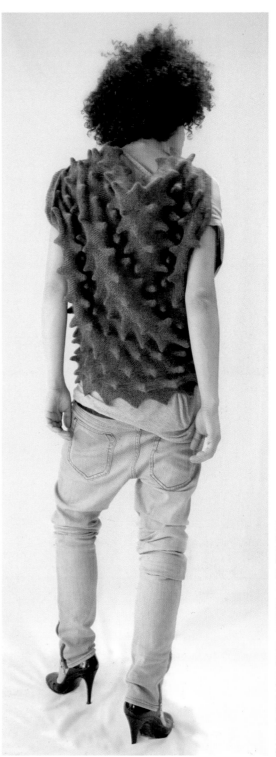

© Laura Delisse López. Design: matalafria; model: Silvia Matas

CONCEPT BOOK OR THEMATIC PANEL

Once the references have been selected and the lines and themes to be explored in the future collection analyzed, the next step is to develop the gathered material in the form of a thematic panel or concept book. This tool allows for expressing through images and key words the overall idea that is to be transmitted in the collection, that is, the compendium of values and symbols that represent it: ideas, feelings, visual references, environments, colors, music, important figures, etc. In addition, by representing, visualizing, and put-ting into writing—whether abstractly or concretely—the references that have served as sources of inspiration, it is possible to better manage the idea of the brand, line, or collection. This guide creates a symbolic universe that serves as the overarching context of the creation. It helps to define the placement of the message or messages that will be developed further in the product, establishing a particular manner of communication and defining the strategy that will be followed with the contribution of a concrete stylistic filter.

The objective is a comprehensive piece that permits taking the design

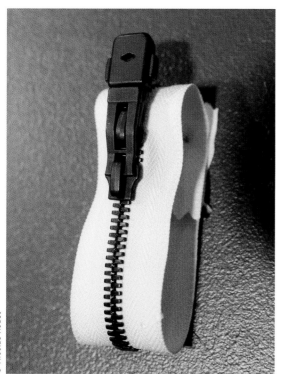

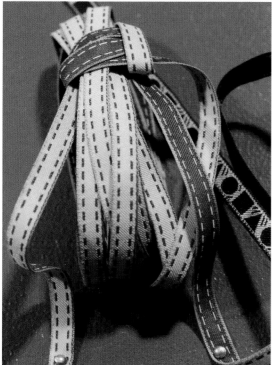

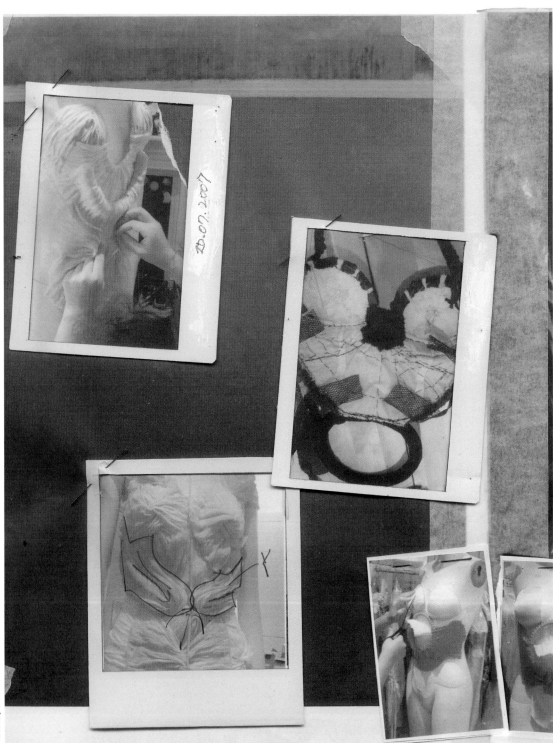

© Steve J & Yoni P

work beyond the creator or designer originally responsible for it. It should function as a guide on the basis of which anyone can develop the collection, which itself may consist of different product lines and/or accessories, graphic applications, or prints.

In addition to the concrete applications of the designer or design team, the concept book helps make the symbolic development of the intangible values and spirit of a collection clear to other teams involved in the process.

The structural framework that should be considered in the elaboration of a concept book is broad, although certain guidelines help to process the information:

- Title
- Justification of the selected positioning
- Thematic philosophy
- List of concrete references (development of the values and the character of the collection)
- Representation of the type of public the collection is aimed at
- Color proposal
- Proposal of garment types
- Proposal of materials
- Development techniques of the garments
- Proposal of types of finishes
- Accessories
- Proposal of style and image and complements

All these guidelines are obtained with the assistance of the following resources, which should be duly examined:
- Text
- Image
- Drawing
- Music (in the case of audiovisual material)

The final step in the development of a concept book or thematic panel consists of producing a graphic unification in a single piece, which can be presented in different formats:
- A book
- A poster or a collage on a rigid support
- An animation
- A short film
- A digital presentation

Once the guidelines of the collection have been defined and realized, it is necessary to develop the specific garments that will conform to them. The most commonly used method for doing so involves fashion figures.

THE FASHION FIGURE

This is a two-dimensional representation of a certain look or garment.

A fashion figure should, above all, appropriately show the fundamental qualities of what it is intended to represent; that is, accurately represent the silhouette, colors, textures, etc. It is important to know that it is not necessary to be an expert illustrator in order to be able to express an idea on paper. A fashion figure does not have to be a fashion illustration, it only needs to be clear about what it is you want to express.

PROPORTIONS

In order to properly draw a fashion figure, it is necessary to know the proportions of the human body and the relations between its parts. The human body is divided into three main blocks: the head, the trunk (which runs from the shoulders to the pubis) and the extremities (legs and arms). The total height of a person is equivalent to eight times the length of the head, although in fashion representation the measure of nine heads is used so as to achieve a more stylized figure; each of these measures is a module.

If a vertical line is drawn along each module and some horizontal lines in its halves and quarters, it is possible to locate all the points needed for drawing a completely proportional

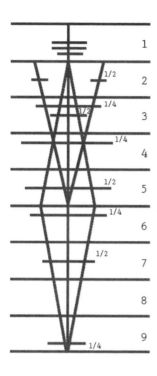

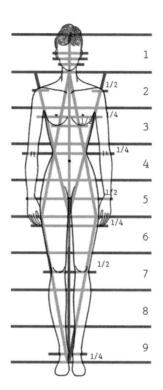

human figure.

POSES

Fashion figures seek to transmit the spirit of a collection. Thus, they are rarely drawn in a rigid or straight posture but rather in a pose that reflects a particular attitude. The simplest way to draw these poses is to combine the trunk and pelvis as trapezoids, the extremities as straight lines, and to indicate the joints, which are fundamental for producing movement, with dots. The result is that these geometric figures turn in relation to their connections while the measure of their lines and proportions is maintained. For example, in a figure drawn

in a state of rest with the hand on the waist, the trapezoid that corresponds to the pelvis sways but does not change its form, which has an effect on the position of the lines that represent the legs. Keeping these norms in mind, and with a little bit of practice, it will be easy to depict any movement, at all times generated from the points of articulation.

REPRESENTATION TECHNIQUES

Different illustration techniques can be employed in the production of a fashion figure: pencil, watercolor, felt-tip pen, mixed techniques, digital support,

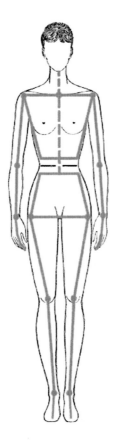
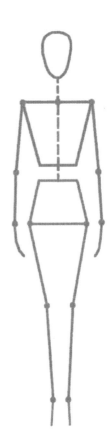

or collage. Each of these techniques contributes a distinct spirit to the representation, and thus the designer will choose one in accordance with what is most convenient for the expression of his or her ideas and the concept of the collection, as well as with what is deemed most comfortable at the time. With the fashion figures completed, and consequently all the pieces that will make up the collection defined, the next step is the production of technical specifications for each of the garments.

TECHNICAL SPECIFICATION

This is a document that depicts the quartering of the garments of a fashion figure in technical drawings (plans) drawn to scale, specifying all the elements and characteristics of which it is composed, such as length, accessories, interlinings, kinds of finishes, etc. Along with the design plan, various color options or fabric samples are included that can be

(continued on p.82)

担当 :

ITEM NO. 12D - 04	TITLE
STYLE F	B

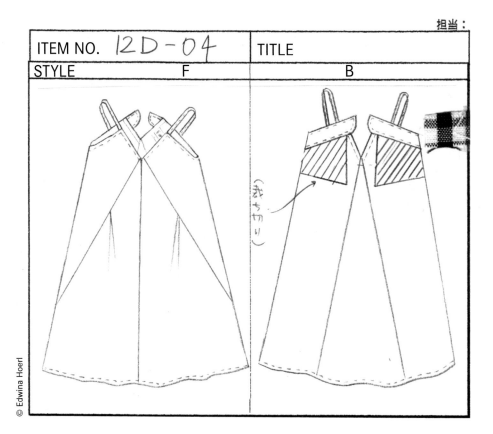

used in the production of the piece. The aim of a technical specification is to make the interpretation of the design easier for the pattern designer or clothes maker and subsequent manufacturing of the garment.

THE PATTERN

With the invention of the sewing machine in 1830, the creative process of fashion began to be industrialized, and it was therefore necessary to come up with a system for producing garments on a massive scale following a set of standard measures that were then adjusted to consumers. Thus patterns were born, in short time becoming very popular among both tailors and consumers of clothes. The use of patterns was also influential in the sense that garments started to be appreciated more for their form and cut than any adornments that might be added to them.

It could be said that patterns are the architecture of fashion, to the extent that they are geometric constructions based on the measures of the body that are used as forms in the production of garments; in other words, they are two-dimensional pieces that

Season	Collection	Detail
Pre/Winter 2006	PRINCESA	NB124

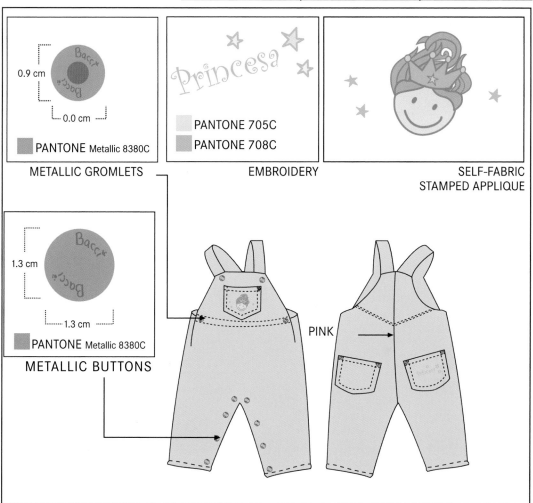

METALLIC GROMLETS

EMBROIDERY

SELF-FABRIC
STAMPED APPLIQUE

0.9 cm
0.0 cm

PANTONE Metallic 8380C

PANTONE 705C
PANTONE 708C

1.3 cm
1.3 cm

PANTONE Metallic 8380C

METALLIC BUTTONS

PINK

PINK 05

EMBROIDERY
COLOR

PANTONE 708C
PANTONE 705C

SEAM COLOR

PANTONE 705C

STAMP
COLOR

70% PANTONE 708C
PANTONE 4725C
70% PANTONE 4725C
PANTONE 708C
PANTONE 290C

Attention
Review Pantone
Specifications
Because the color in
monitor and impressions
are not the real ones

 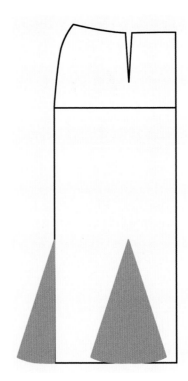

reflect the three-dimensional nature of a garment. Each pattern consists of all the pieces that go into a garment, and the larger the number of pieces the more complex the composition of the design will be. For example, the pattern for a jacket will include the pieces for the back, the front, the sleeves, the collar, the pockets, the facings, and the lining, thus qualifying it as a rather complex garment to produce. It is important to keep in mind that all of these pieces are part of a unit, and as such if one piece is modified this will affect all the others, which, in turn, will require modification as well. Preciseness in patterns is fundamental to arriving at a well-made garment that feels good to wear.

There exist basic design patterns for skirts, jackets, pants, etc., which, in order to obtain new volumes, can be taken as a base and with the application of pleats, cloth inserts, and reductions of cloth, can be played with to create garments that are much more innovative and elaborate. It is striking how the variation of small elements sometimes can change the image of a garment completely. A simple example of this is the skirt shown in the image, which with the insertion of godets and some pleats, goes from being a piece with a totally straight silhouette to one with volume and movement.

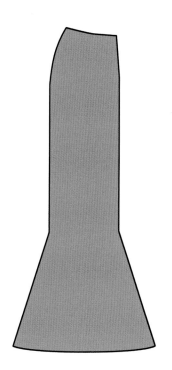
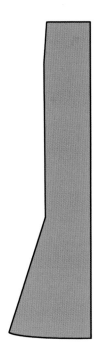

Patterns are generally drawn on paper, preferably paper with a certain amount of resistance but also easy to cut. Some people prefer semi-transparent paper in order to be able to modify the drawing with greater ease.

Once the pattern is finished and any modifications deemed necessary have been carried out, the pieces are then cut individually. As a reference for knowing where to join one with the other, or where to make a mark or fold in the cloth later on, small holes are made in the cloth.

To transfer the pattern to the fabric, it is necessary to have washed the cloth—to avoid possible deformations such as shrinking—and ironed it. It is then positioned upside down, and the pieces of the pattern are set on top of it, keeping in mind the orientation of the motifs or, if present, the texture of the fabric, as in the case of corduroy. In such cases the pieces can only be placed in one direction so that they look right when joined together, which perhaps prevents taking advantage of the entire surface of the cloth and will require that more of it be bought than if the cloth were solid and without any printing on it.

Once they have been used, patterns are stored in envelopes or hung from hooks, in order to avoid wrinkling.

THE *MOULAGE*

This is a technique that consists in the three-dimensional creation of a design or pattern, molding the fabric directly onto a body, whether it be the body of a sewing dummy or a model. For this reason it might be said that it is a form of "sculpting on a body with cloth."

Despite being an artisanal process, it is a technique that allows for the creation of atypical volumes that would be very difficult to obtain one-dimensionally. This characteristic makes it a technique utilized rather frequently in haute couture, and some designers of prêt-à-porter also employ it in the creation of certain garments.

THE TEST GARMENT

This is the first sample of the garment once the pattern has been developed. Generally it is done with calico, percale, or some other fabric with the same weight and behavior as the fabric that will be used for the final garment, as it is possible that a pattern will not function with a fabric different from the one for which it has been conceived. For instance, if the fabric to be used for the garment is elastic, a knit fabric must be used for the test garment. Normally, the fabric is white or natural, given that these colors make the cuts and tailoring of the pattern easier to see.

In this first sample, it is not necessary to sew the lining or the pockets. Only the elements involved in the construction of the garment are made, so as to be able to visualize the piece in three dimensions prior to its construction. Thus, it is possible to fine-tune the proportions and details, as well as to confirm that the pattern is properly made and the garment adapts well to the body. In the case of the latter, it is at this time that corrections must be made and the garment modified, which can be executed directly onto the test garment with tailor's chalk. Once all the changes have been made the corrections must then be incorporated into the patterns.

© Txell Miras. Design: Txell Miras. AW 2005-2006 at Passarella Gaudí

THE PROTOTYPE

The final step in the creative process is to make a prototype, that is, a version of the garment as it will later appear at retail respecting fabrics, colors, finishes, etc. Normally, prototypes are used as a sample of the collection on fashion runways and in the press, and are therefore generally made in size 36 or 38 in order to fit the models.

Once the prototype is completed, the developmental process of a collection is over and the time has come to present it, to offer it to possible buyers, to begin production, and follow the necessary steps so that the garments actually will be able to be worn.

GLOSSARY

Accessories: decorative or fastening complementary pieces on a dress garment.

Analogous range: harmonious range created from two or three colors closely situated in the chromatic circle.

Artificial fibers: fibers that come from natural elements but are subjected to industrial transformation processes.

Blog: log published on the Internet, updated periodically by its author or authors.

Collage: artistic technique consisting of creating a composition that includes elements of a diverse nature.

Color: refers to the hue or tone itself.

Complementary range: harmonious range formed by two complementary colors and their shades.

Concept book: also called a thematic panel, a tool that helps give expression to the ideas a collection wants to transmit through images and key words.

Continuous fabric: method used to obtain cloth and knit fabrics.

Discontinuous fabric: method for obtaining nonfabrics.

Fashion figure: two-dimensional representation of a look or garment.

Gadget: element with a specific purpose and function, practical and at the same time novel.

Interlining: hidden element that provides form and support in specific areas of a garment.

Knit fabric: cloth made up of loops of knit thread.

Length: meters per kilogram of a thread or fabric.

Monochromatic range: harmonious range obtained with a single color by varying its saturation and/or value.

Moulage: technique consisting in the creation of a three-dimensional design or pattern, molding the fabric directly onto the body of a model or sewing dummy.

Nanotechnology: scientific discipline concerned with the control and manipulation of material on a scale inferior to one micrometer (at the atomic and molecular level).

Natural fibers: fibers made from animal, plant, or mineral components.

Nonfabrics: cloths produced from the compression of fabrics via heat, friction, or chemical products.

Pattern: geometric construction based on the measurements of the figure used as a model for producing garments.

Prototype: version of a garment as it will later appear at the point of sale.

Saturation: degree of intensity of a color.

Sketchbook: a notebook that reflects the creative process of a garment or collection of a designer.

Synthetic fibers: fibers produced entirely from chemical products.

Test garment: first sample of a garment, generally made with white or natural-colored fabric.

Thematic panel: *see* concept book.

Value: degree of brightness or darkness of a color.

Vintage clothing: quality clothes that are out of season and considered classic.

PRODUCTION

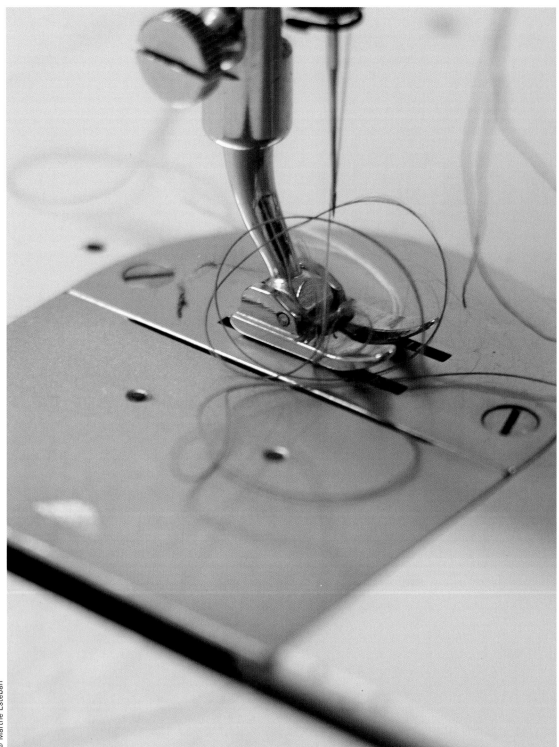

PRODUCTION

Fashion is a business that moves quickly and operates at a dizzying pace: it must supply the market with new products constantly—every four to six months—in addition to being global and extremely competitive.

It is for this reason that a fashion designer must not only conceive of collections, but also be familiar with all the processes involved in their creation. By doing so, they are subsequently able to meet the demands of the market and produce what has been planned in conformity with corresponding times and periods.

The majority of designers that are just starting out in the world of fashion usually do not have the capital needed to form a solid team to deal with matters of management and production. This means that the designer herself must possess sufficient knowledge to be able to carry out not only the design aspect of the project, but also to be in charge of the production, marketing, sales, and logistics departments. This requires knowing something about economics, understanding the evolution of the market and consumption, and being familiar with the way one's industry functions.

CHAINS OF PRODUCTION

In the industrial process of production there are two large chains: the textile-clothing chain and the leather, complements, and footwear chain. These are the two avenues that connect designers to suppliers, who will work harder and perform better the closer the relationship is between the two.

Knowing and understanding the links in each chain is fundamental for understanding how the industry works. If one wants to increase the speed, quality, and efficiency of production, one must be familiar and agile with each process in the chain.

The basic outline of textile-clothing production is: fibers, spinning, knitting, finishing, and clothing.

The basic outline of the leather-complements-footwear chain is: tanning, finishing, and manufacturing.

More or less in stages, both cases involve choosing raw materials, deciding how they will be treated, and then producing samples. As both chains nowadays are structured on a global scale, large production or manufac-

turing volumes can be carried out at economical prices in developing countries in Eastern Europe, the Mediterranean region, and Asia. The rest of Europe, on the other hand, has come to specialize in high-end limited series, that is, in complex and expensive procedures which, for this reason, are difficult to copy.

PURCHASE OF RAW MATERIALS

Fabrics and accessories are the raw materials of the garments that make up a collection, and as such play an important role in its production. A poor fabric can dash a spectacular design while, conversely, an excellent fabric can invest a mediocre design with quality.

Being aware of innovations in the textile market can also prove very useful, since a fabric with certain properties can occasionally contribute to increasing the value of the garment, apart from its design. However, to what extent the value is increased must be kept in mind, taking into consideration whether the consumer will ultimately be willing to pay the elevated price. Experts indicate that the cost of raw materials should not exceed 30 percent of the total production of the collection.

© Dorotea

The leather industry has the inconvenience of being a market sector with a more limited offer than the fabric sector, since it is a business dependent upon cattle. In Europe, for example, the practical disappearance of the primary economy—based on agriculture and ranching—has had an impact on leather. Countries that stand out as suppliers of quality leather are India and Brazil.

Innovation is equally important in this field especially regarding methods that grant leather more flexibility, lightness, resistance, and softness, although obtaining new textures and colors is also valued.

In the case of footwear, in addition to leather and accessories, it is also necessary to purchase other components such as soles and heels that play a crucial role in the final design.

To access suppliers of raw materials, one can turn to an association of textile businesses or simply attend a textile fair.

TEXTILE FAIRS

Fairs are events organized annually or biannually with the aim of promoting a fashion sector where the main manufacturers and suppliers have the opportunity to show their products in exhibitions or stands, gaining new clients in

RAW MATERIALS FAIR CALENDAR

Fairs	Seasons
Pitti Immagine Filati (yarns and latest trends), Florence	January–February 2009
	Spring–Summer 2010
Milano Unica (fabrics), Milan	September 2009
Prèmiere Vision Pluriel, Paris	Fall–Winter 2010-2011
Texworld (fabrics), Paris	
Munich Fabric Start (fabrics), Munich	

the process. They are held in January and February to meet the supply needs of spring and summer collections and in September for fall and winter collections of the following year. This means that innovations and trends in raw materials are known eighteen months before the consumer can acquire the finished garment from the store.

The most important fairs in Europe are the Prèmiere Vision Pluriel, which takes place in Paris and includes Prèmiere Vision for fabrics, Expofil for fabrics and yarns, Mod'Amont for accessories, and Le cuir a Paris for leather; Pitti Immagine Filati in Florence for yarns and latest trends, and fairs devoted exclusively to fabrics such as Milano Unica, Munich Fabric Start and Texworld, in Paris, which brings in Asian weavers.

Navigating a fair is not easy, especially the first time around. Prèmiere Vision, for example, brings together around 700 exhibitors, and it is practically impossible to visit them all. The most practical thing to do is to begin with the latest-trends show. It provides information about fabric proposals for the upcoming season, with samples accompanied by the name of the manufacturer, and thus can serve as a point of departure.

PURCHASING ALTERNATIVES

Aside from fairs, another option consists of contacting distributors or agents, businesses that work with different manufacturers. Sometimes this proves an attractive alternative because an intermediary can facilitate the process. Through direct contact with the manufacturer, prices can be negotiated according to amounts, as the intermediary customarily works with various designers or different brands.

For a first contact, another useful resource is the Internet, with its specialized pages for searching for raw materials.

THE SUPPLIERS

Whether one chooses to do so through associations, fairs, distributors or agents, the most complicated decision

is where and how to buy, for it is a choice that involves many factors and entails the manufacturer becoming the supplier to the designer. This is true both of the textile and leather sectors, with an added difficulty in the latter case: leather is an expensive material.

A good and close relationship between the supplier and the designer is essential, whether one is just starting out or has already made a name for oneself. In fact, designers now refer to suppliers as partners or collaborators given that they are partly responsible for a designer's success. In the case of luxury brands, for instance, suppliers are one of the brand's main assets, as the two often develop collections consisting of exclusive fabrics together, not only to surprise clients, but also to avoid copies.

When buying the materials it is necessary to know the amount of fabric needed for the entire collection. At the outset of negotiations, the first thing that the weaver will demand is an order for a minimum of meters. So if a designer does not have a large production in mind, it is advisable for her to buy a large quantity of a limited range of fabrics. It must be remembered that the less meters ordered, the more difficult it will be to negotiate prices and, consequently, the more expensive the fabric will be. Occasionally, one finds surplus fabric or fabrics from other seasons in stock, at lower prices. In footwear, moreover, it is difficult to calculate the amount of meters needed because the shoe production process is very complex.

Once the order is made, it is advisable to stay in touch with the supplier and, once received, to make sure the delivery corresponds with the order.

In any event, between the time of the negotiation of amounts, prices, and delivery dates and the reception of the order, it is normal to maintain contact in order to manage possible modifications and ensure agreement down to the smallest detail that might have been overlooked, such as who will be responsible for shipping costs, the suppler or the designer, something that should be reflected in the invoice.

During this period it is also important to control the duration of time in the processes as any delay in the arrival of the fabric can have an impact on the timely arrival of the garment to the store. This delay can result in the piece not appearing in the shop window, its missing out on the beginning of the season, or remaining in the warehouse until sales.

TEXTILE ENNOBLING

Also known as finishing, it is present in the textile-clothing and leather production chains, bringing together all the processes to which raw materials—fiber, thread, fabric, cloth, and warp-knit cloth—are subjected to the different stages of production, such as dyeing, printing, and bleaching. It must be kept in mind that, depending on the design, a garment can require a specific ennobling subsequent to production, such as giving it an aged look or adding embroidery to the design.

These processes are extremely important because on the one hand they help distinguish between fabrics and on the other they increase their value, allowing fabrics to adapt to the functional needs of fashion—always in a constant state of change and evolution.

Because the same fabric sometimes involves different finishing procedures, it is common for weavers to work hand in hand with companies that specialize in textile ennobling. These tend to be smaller than those devoted to textile production, with a more diversified selection and less automated work method.

While the designer should be familiar with this aspect of production, direct involvement in the process is not necessary, unless development of a particular kind of fabric is desired.

Below are some of the main ennobling processes.

DYEING

This process involves submerging the textile in a coloring-solution bath mixed with fixers and mordant dyes. This combination, along with the time the cloth remains in the bath, allows the color to be soaked up by the fabric, fusing with it completely and thus altering the original tone of the material. There is also a procedure called reserve dyeing in which a part of the cloth is withheld from the dye. The

dye-free section retains the fabric's original color, allowing for different shapes, gradation, and effects on the cloth. The most common techniques are tie-dyeing and batik, a method in which areas of reserve cloth are covered with wax.

BLEACHING

Bleaching consists of immersing the fabric in a hot bath with a bleaching solution, which is then absorbed through a combination of hydrophobic interactions. However, the use of the fabric and the bathing processes slowly give rise to the inverse process, de-absorption, and therefore once the garment has been made, the use of detergents that contain bleaching agents is recommended.

PRINTS

This is the process of transferring an image onto a fabric. It can be a concrete image, which will be situated in a specific part of the garment, or a full print, where the entire cloth is printed with a repeating pattern.

Design: jasmin shokrian. AW 2007-2008, *The other side of something else.*
Courtesy of Photogenics Media

Printing can be carried out with rollers, blocks, heat transference, warp, corrosion, or silk screening.

DRESSINGS

They are used as a finishing for leather garments as way of protecting them from scratching, wear, and abrasion. They form a more or less hard, shiny film with high resistance to friction, and therefore have a direct influence on the look and feel of the leather.

COLLECTION OF SAMPLES

The production of prototypes or samples is the most expensive part of this first stage of production, as well as one that involves a good deal of risk since it is possible that not all of the designs will be received positively by clients. Only what is to be sold will be sent off for production, always taking into account surplus in case the store needs to resupply mid-season.

The process is exhausting, since the market demands at least three collections per season: the main collection, the pre-collection, flash collections, and updates. Until relatively recently, a collection every six months, coinciding with the two seasons, was sufficient.

Once the sale has been made, the next step is grading the prototypes that will be produced. It is therefore essential to be clear about who the design is for, whether for a woman, a man, or a child, as sizes vary.

SIZE TABLES FOR CLOTHES

Women

Pants

United Kingdom	S	S	M	M	L	L	XL
United States	4	6	8	10	12	14	16
Europe	34	36	38	40	42	44	46
Measurement in cm	64-67	68-70	70-72.5	73-75	76-78	79-82	83-86

Blouses, tops, jackets

United Kingdom (letters)	XXS	XS	S	M	L	XL	XXL
United Kingdom	6	8	10	12	14	16	18
United States	0	2	4	6	8	10	12
Europe	34	36	38	40	42	44	46
Measurement in cm	85-87.5	88-90	90.5-92.5	93-96	96.5-99	99.5-103	103.5-107

Men

Pants

United Kingdom/United States	28	30	32	34	36	38	40
Europe	38	40	42	44	46	48	50
Measurement in cm	71-75	76-79	80-85	86-90	91-94	95-99	100-105

Shirts

United Kingdom/United States	14	14	15	15	16	16	17
Europe	36	37	38	39	41	42	43

Suits, sweaters, coats

United Kingdom/United States	32	34	36	38	40	42	44
Europe	42	44	46	48	50	52	54

Children

Size	XS	S	S-M	M	M-L	L	L-XL
Age	4	6-8	8-10	10	10-12	12	12-14
Height in cm	104	116	128	140	152	158	164

SIZE TABLES FOR SHOES

Women

United Kingdom	3	3.5	4	4.5	5	5.5	6	6.5	7	7.5				
United States	5.5	6	6.5	7	7.5	8	8.5	9	9.5	10				
Europe	36.5	37	37.5	38	38.5	39	39.5	40	41	41.5				
Measurement in cm	22.5	23	23.5	24	24.5	25	25.5	26	26.5	27				

Men

United Kingdom	5.5	6	6.5	7	7.5	8	8.5	9	9.5	10	10.5	11	12	13
United States	6.5	7	7.5	8	8.5	9	9.5	10	10.5	11	11.5	12	13	14
Europe	39	40	40.5	41	41.5	42	42.5	43	43.5	44	44.5	45	46	47
Measurement in cm	24.5	25	25.5	26	26.5	27	27.5	28	28.5	29	29.5	30	31	32

© Rachel Meginnes. Michael Cepress at his Studio/Showroom

PATTERN GRADING

This process is carried out with the aim of acquiring different sizes for a single design, covering the entire range of sizes offered by the market in which the collection is to be sold. This is done mainly by rearranging certain stitches of the outline of each of the pieces that make up the basic pattern of the garment, which may or may not affect other internal stitching of the designs.

Throughout this process the role of the pattern designer is of utmost importance. The pattern designer is a professional that works alongside the designer and is responsible for developing both the original pattern and the grading, indicating the materials and exact accessories for each piece.

Once the specific materials and the grading have been indicated for the garment, the design is ready to be sent to the workshop for production.

CALCULATION OF COSTS

Before undertaking the collection of samples, once the general lines of the collection and its designs have been defined, a planning template should be drawn up, with a sales forecast by product classes, in order to keep track of the materials that will be needed and their costs.

This template consists of the different technical specifications for each garment, indicating such information as the kind of fabric, length, color, and sizes, which is helpful in the calculation of the consumption of fabrics and other materials as well as the approximate cost over sales forecasts.

From the planning template two other templates are obtained: one for the collection of samples, with instructions for the production of the sample and its costs, and the production template, with information concerning measurements and materials.

To calculate exact costs it is necessary to know the measurements of the garments, and the number of pieces of each one. The more complex the pattern of the garments, the more costly and difficult the production processes. If the designer is over budget when it comes time to buy the fabric, she can compensate by simplifying the pattern. However, if one has been prudent with the use of raw materials, the collection can increase in value with the choice of a more elaborate pattern.

When negotiating with the workshop hired to carry out mass production of the garments, such matters as production volume, variety, and variability—the variables of each garment in terms of color, accessories, etc.—must be kept in mind. The greater the volume, the more leeway one has to negotiate a lower price; on the other hand, the more variety and variability, the higher the expenses as this adds complexity to the collection in addition to lengthening delivery times.

PRODUCTION

Finding a good workshop is not easy. In recent years, the textile and clothing industries have been in a state of crisis, and this has had an impact on all markets. For example, in Europe, with delocalization, manufacturing above all has been affected; with the number of workshops diminished. The ones that remain find themselves overwhelmed. For this reason, as in the rest of the production process, it is important to monitor delivery times, for if a production order is not very high, the workshop can push it

COST TEMPLATE

Total fabric cost

Type ....
Cost/meter ....
Total length cost ....
Fabric 1 ....
Fabric 2 ....
Linings ....
Shipping ....
Others ....

Total accessories cost

Type ....
Cost/unit ....
Total units ....
Total cost ....

Buttons ....
Zippers ....
Ribbons ....
Labels ....
Others ....

Total manufacture cost

Cost ....
Grading ....
Cut ....
Stitching ....
Workshop ....

Total reception cost

Cost ....
Shipping ....
Warehousing ....

Final price estimate
Total production cost

+ Agent/representative cost ....
+ Agent/representative margin ....
+ Store margin ....

© Jorge Andreu. Design: Gori de Palma. AW 2009-2010 at 080 Barcelona Fashion

to the back of the line behind larger production orders of other clients, thus jeopardizing the pre-established delivery time.

Also complicating matters, especially for young designers or emerging brands, is that, like suppliers, workshops require a minimum production volume. It is important to negotiate effectively and, as with suppliers of raw materials, to establish clearly who is responsible for shipping and what the delivery times are, specifying whether shipments will be made in a single block at the end of production or in various phases. As for the collection, it is necessary to specify

all details so that no errors occur during production. One must be meticulous, not taking anything for granted. Any oversight, no matter how small, can be disastrous and irreversible. It is necessary to send all information to the workshop in a clear manner, detailing the designs, sizes, and colors of each garment.

Opening the boxes with the finished garments inside is always a moment of suspense: One can find children's jeans instead of men's, wrinkled shirts, unequal sleeves, irregular seams, and more. It is for this reason that quality control is so essential, involving frequent contact with

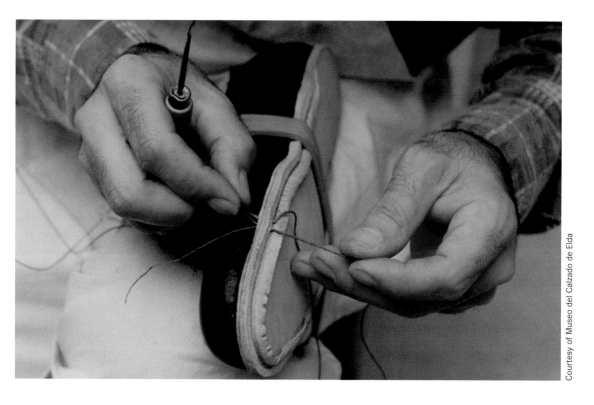

the workshop in order to supervise how production is progressing. If one neglects to do this until the garments are finished, the outcome may be unpleasant, with irreparable surprises. That said, it is worth mentioning that marketing has turned some of these mistakes into successes—for example, snow jeans—but since this is not a universal law, and one does not always have the luxury of a marketing department, it is better to avoid such errors, requesting from the workshop samples of the garments and making corrections as one goes along. This sort of management is necessary if one wishes to avoid arguments after the fact about who is responsible for

the mistake. Something can always go overlooked, but the objective is that prior to packaging, one have the certainty that no big surprises await at the other end.

This is one of the problems of manufacturing abroad. Producing in North Africa or China may be cheaper, but if one lacks the resources for close quality control, the choice may ultimately turn out to be a mistake.

In the production of footwear, the process is even more complicated. A shoe consists of many pieces, and limited series are very expensive. Thus, the prototype for a shoe is costly

PRODUCTION CALENDAR

Month	Fall-Winter	Spring-Summer
July-August I	Ideas, design of the collection	
September-October	Selection, ordering of fabrics	
November	Patterns, first samples	
December	Development of collection of sample	
January	End of collection, start of sales	Ideas, design of collection
February-March	Presentation of collection, sales	Selection, ordering of fabrics
April	Ordering of fabrics and accessories	Patterns, first samples
May	Start of production	Development of collection of samples
June	Production	End of collection, start of sales
July-August	End of production, start of deliveries	Presentation of collection, sales
September-October	Deliveries, payments	Presentation of collection, sales
November		Ordering of fabrics and accessories
December		Start of production
January		Production
February		End of production, start of deliveries
March-April		Deliveries, payments

and, in addition, two are required, one for each foot. The same holds true when negotiating with a workshop to produce the collection. Workshops do not accept small orders, and the minimums they demand seem very high if one is working with a small budget. This is why in these cases it is common to work with fabrics or plastics as opposed to leather, as the bulk of the cost falls on manufacturing.

WAREHOUSE

In addition to controlling delivery times, it is essential to know where the delivery is to be made. Normally, deliveries are sent to agreed-upon places such as the designer's studio or a business establishment
Specialized external warehouses exist that are used by brands that work with large volumes and various workshops. In this case, it is the warehouse that is responsible for classifying the garments by client and shipping them.

Since fashion is cyclical, the warehouse will only be full during decisive periods of production, while between seasons it will remain practically empty.

CALENDAR

Familiarity with the calendar is indispensable in a business in which tardiness is simply not an option. It might seem complicated (as the sales of one collection come to a close, work on the next one is already underway), but it is simply a matter of being systematic about one's work.

Prêt-à-porter, compared to other sectors, such as haute couture and large-scale distribution, has a programmed calendar around which the entire industry is structured, and on the basis of which the entire textile-clothing chain operates.

Until now, this calendar included two collections per year, the spring-summer and fall-winter collections. Today, however, there are six, including main collections, precollections and updates, with the aim of offering better service to stores and seducing the consumer with constant novelty.

PRODUCTION MANAGEMENT

For managing production one must create an easy system to calculate the value of a collection and all the processes a collection involves. The classic way of estimating costs is to add up all the materials—fabrics, accessories, patterns, and others—and indicate the cost of each process.

Also on the market are different software management tools for the production of fashion collections. While requiring a significant investment, they compensate in the long run since effort in this area can be avoided each season. They are very advanced programs that help to develop not only the design of a garment, but also the patterns and grading, allowing for precise calculation of costs. Fashion brands, for example, tend to incorporate these design and pattern software tools via computers, applying the information they contain to machines that cut different patterns from the fabric. In this way, maximum use can be made of the cloth, keeping waste at a minimum.

Lastly, it is worth mentioning that in fashion the final sales price of the garment is not calculated by adding the total cost to the profit margin of the designer and the margins of the agents and stores. When setting the price, a series of intangible elements, albeit with a tangible cost, is considered, such as the image of the brand, which in some cases is the reason why the price of a garment is much higher than the cost of its production.

The forecasts made in this chapter apply only to production. Next, one must distribute the collection to the market, communicate it, and advertise it.

GLOSSARY

Batik: reserve dyeing technique involving the use of wax.

Bleaching: type of finish consisting of the immersion of the fabric in a warm bath with a bleaching agent.

Collection of samples: samples or prototypes of a collection.

Dressings: finishing for leather.

Dyeing: process by which a textile changes its original color after being submerged in a bath containing a coloring solution combined with fixers and mordant dyes.

Finishing: also called textile ennobling, includes all the processes involving raw materials in the different stages of their processing.

Full print: print made on the entire surface of the cloth.

Logistics: means and resources that allow an activity to be carried out.

Management software: computer programs that help to develop the design of a garment, create patterns and gradations, and make a precise calculation of costs.

Marketing: techniques that, through market studies, seek to obtain maximum benefit from the sale of product.

Partner: associate.

Pattern designer: professional who works with the designer, responsible for developing both the original pattern and the gradation.

Pattern grading: process carried out to obtain different sizes of the same design.

Planning template: control template for materials needed in the production of a collection and their respective costs.

Prèmiere Vision Pluriel: main textile fair held in Paris.

Primary economy: economy based on agriculture and ranching.

Printing: process of transferring an image onto a textile.

Supplier: person or company that supplies stock.

Reserve dyeing: dyeing method in which part of the cloth is withheld from the dye and retains its original color.

Tanning: refers to furs and leather.

Textile ennobling: *see* finishing.

Textile fair: event organized annually or biannually with the purpose of promoting a fashion sector.

Tie-dyeing: reserve dyeing technique involving the use of strings, straps, etc.

Warehouse: place where garments are stored prior to being distributed to points of sale.

SALES AND DISTRIBUTION

SALES AND DISTRIBUTION

SALES PROCESS

With the collection developed and the collection of samples completed, the next step is to begin the sales process for the collection and decide where and how it should be distributed.

For carrying out sales, a designer has two ways to gain access to the market: through her own store, which is the best way to have direct contact with consumers—to know their opinion and learn which garments they like most and which ones they like least—and through multi-brand stores, which for a designer just starting out is the simplest way of getting her foot in the door. How to reach these stores depends on the resources the designer has. It may be done personally, which involves extra work, such as visiting the parts of cities where one is most interested in being, researching existing stores, deciding in which stores the collection best fits, and, finally, making contact with the stores. This can also be done with the help of a professional, through the hiring of an agent or a sales representative.

THE AGENT OR SALES REPRESENTATIVE

This is a sales professional who knows the sector and understands how distribution functions in certain regions or countries. His goal is to bring the collection or brand of a designer to multi-brand stores, acting as an intermediary between the point of sale and the designer, and charging a commission of around 10 percent on any sales made. A good agent should not only have good interpersonal skills, but also should understand the collection, believe in the designer's project or brand, know the establishments most suited for selling the collection, and be able to effectively close a deal. The goal is not only to sell the collection, but also sell it in the right place.

Agents or representatives tend to have a client portfolio, that is, various brands and designers with whom to negotiate possible sales and stipulate volumes, deliveries, and prices. Some choose to diversify their portfolio rather widely in order to avoid having clients coincide in the same market sector, while others prefer to specialize in concrete areas and thus often work with a network of very specific stores, offering a broad range of options within a single motif or style.

As the distribution market tends toward specialization according to styles and the diversification of products, the second strategy is more advisable. In any case, it is not a general rule.

When it comes time to select an agent it is essential to have a clear idea of where one wants to sell—cities, regions, types of stores, etc.—therefore, the professional to be chosen will not simply be the one who is the most enthusiastic about the project but one whose sphere of activity is in tune with the established strategy.

The designer-agent relationship should be a close one, as the agent is the intermediary between the designer and the consumer. The agent is not only responsible for order placement in the stores, but also for gathering the impressions of the store owners or managers, which means that he is the first person to know if people like the collection, if it fits within the chosen market sector, if it is a success, if there are elements that need to be strengthened, if any lines could be discontinued, etc. Designers or brands that have their own stores receive this information firsthand and almost immediately, which allows them to act fast. With an intermediary agent, however, contact with the point of sale and the consumer is diluted. To avoid this, it is necessary to build a relationship based on mutual trust and teamwork.

The agent is responsible for communicating the response obtained from the market and offering suggestions. According to the requests made by store owners or managers, the agent can even call for changes to be made to the collection. All such proposals should be carefully measured and considered. As it is impossible for a brand or designer to control the sales pitch used by the agent or representative when negotiating with stores, it is extremely important to establish the limits of these negotiations, agreeing with the agent from the start about

© Jorge Andreu. Conference of Lutz, SS 2009 at 080 Barcelona Fashion

what is negotiable and what is not, and to what point. Any modification can increase the cost of production, or simply make it unfeasible. Although on certain occasions a change made in time can save a collection, it is also true that some changes can betray the philosophy of the collection or project that has been undertaken.

PRESENTATION OF THE COLLECTION

Once the designer or brand has decided either to work with an agent or act independently, the first step in selling the collection is to present a collection of samples to the purchasing representatives of stores.

It is important to present the collection in accordance with the prêt-à-porter calendar; in other words, January-February for a fall-winter collection and July-September for a spring-summer collection. With the emergence of pre-collections, two new presentation periods have begun to carve a space out for themselves on the calendar: May for intermediate collections between winter and spring, and December for collections that bridge summer and fall.

Presenting designs outside of the established dates can lead to a disaster. If one decides to show a collection early, normally clients are unwilling to take a risk because they are still unaware of new trends, they have yet to see what other designers are presenting, and they have not anticipated the upcoming season yet, etc. Once the final show of Paris Women's Fashion Week is over, everything has been decided. Thus, while presenting early is risky, doing so late is impossible, as all orders have already been made and closed.

The showroom

This is the most common way to present a collection to professional distribution buyers. Showrooms are spaces conceived and designed for selling to stores. Concentrated normally in the same areas of major capitals, they are open during the same dates to facilitate the visit of buyers, usually by prearranged appointment.

If the resources are available, it is ideal to have one's own showroom and invite interested potential clients there to view the garments directly, utilizing a wide range of elements to explain both the collection and the philosophy of the brand. When a designer or brand is just starting out, however, or when one wishes to enter a foreign market, it is more custom-

ary to have recourse to a multi-brand showroom. In many cases, the agent or sales representative has a showroom where she can present collections to store owners or managers.

Showrooms often mimic the stores themselves, with the aim of offering ideas and suggestions about the presentation of the collection. This is far more typical of showrooms that belong to the brand itself, in which everything is carefully controlled, although it is becoming increasingly important in multi-brand showrooms as well, where each collection has its own area and tries to adapt according to its own style. The objective, in any case, is to create a relaxed and personalized work environment.

Despite the fact that the sales calendar is fixed and the presentation space must adhere to it, the showroom is a place always open to obtaining orders, defining changes, and working on intermediate deliveries or repositionings. Also, it is open to stylists, who request garments from a collection for fashion articles, promoting the pieces in magazines or via virtual portals.

Fairs and shows

These are specific sales events. In contrast to a showroom, at a fair a space is rented for a limited time (three or four days, usually) for making contacts and acquiring orders, though not necessarily through prearranged appointments. Brands and designers attend if they do not have a showroom or if they are seeking out new contacts. They accompany the sales agent, who is in charge of selecting the points of sales, making contacts, and negotiating orders. Furthermore, fairs are a good platform for making oneself known, especially to international buyers with whom establishing contact is otherwise difficult. It is an opportunity to present oneself personally, show the collection, and strike up an initial sales relationship.

The range of fairs runs wide, and therefore it is necessary to find one that matches the collection one wishes to sell for it to be a useful framework of presentation. The growing specialization of distribution also makes it obligatory that fairs be organized thematically: urban, feminine, masculine, sports, swimwear, underwear, bridal, or footwear fashion, to name a few, thus making the task of determining which are the most advisable to attend easier. In any case, some fairs are simply a must, whether due to their historical significance or the volume of exhibitors, such as Who's Next, which is held twice a year in Paris.

Men's collections are the first to be shown in Florence, at the Pitti Immagine Uomo show (which now incorporates a section for women's precollections), which then passes the baton on to fashion shows, showrooms, and shows included in Men's Fashion Week Milan and Paris. At the same time, Bread & Butter is held in Berlin, featuring urban fashion collections for both men and women. Then comes women's prêt-à-porter, first in New York, and later in London, Milan, and Paris, respectively. Parallel to the fashion weeks in these cities are other professional fairs held in the majority of European capitals.

Until recently, fairs specializing in shoes, complements, and accessories were celebrated at a later date. Today, however, they tend to follow the same calendar as clothes collections, due to their growing presence in boutiques.

WHO'SNEXT09

INTERNATIONAL FASHION SHOW
29 JAN. – 01st FEV. 2009
PARIS – PORTE DE VERSAILLES
HALL 1
WWW.WHOSNEXT.COM

DIRECTEUR ARTISTIQUE: KAMEL YAHIMI

© BREAD & BUTTER GmbH

© BREAD & BUTTER GmbH

Sieger at Pitti Immagine Uomo

A GENTLEMEN'S COLOUR COLLECTION

FASHION & ACCESSORIES

MAKING THE SALE

Two things will prove to be extremely useful for selling a collection: the lookbook and the catalog of references. These graphic pieces, which the potential buyer can take away from the fair or showroom, go into detail about the collection just seen and thus can help in deciding what and how much to buy.

The lookbook is a tool created for each collection that includes all the garments that make up the collection. These images can be taken from the fashion show or from a design to show the buyer in a clear and direct way how the garment looks when worn and how it might appear as a part of an outfit. Not only does this make the sales pitch stronger, it provides ideas about possible ways of positioning the garment at points of sale.

Each design is referenced, allowing the buyer to indicate what garments she is interested in and, later, to show fashion stylists the garments that will be used in future media insertions.

The other tool, the catalog of references, includes work pages that present a detailed description of each garment, with a drawing or a photograph,

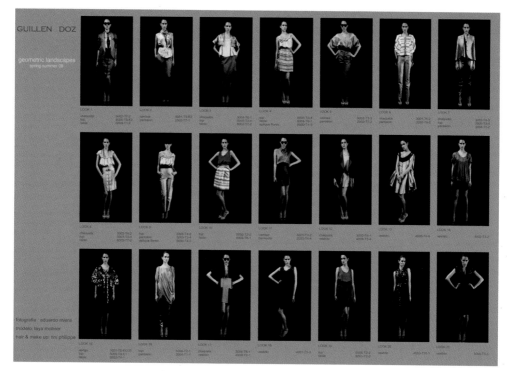

and list of variables—color, fabric and accessories—the price of the garment, its code, and date of delivery.

Prices

When negotiating a sale, price influences to a great extent whether the sale is made or not. It is essential that its appearance in the catalog of references be clear in order to avoid misunderstandings.

As for the designer, the variables to be considered when setting the price of a garment are: the design, the fabric, and in some cases, especially shoes, the size.

The order

Once the client has seen the collection and decided to buy it, the order is then processed. This is a document that details the amount of each design that has been bought, the sizes and colors, the corresponding prices, delivery dates, payments, and possible service penalties.

Delivery dates

When negotiating with stores it is important to agree upon the times and dates of delivery, which will vary according to the country. Meeting these deadlines is as important as the content of a collection. Being late can

PURCHASE ORDER

Name of the designer

Designer's tax information:

Invoice number:

Name of the client: Name of the store:

Tax information: Contact information:

Design	Color	Description	Sizes XS S M L	Units	Price per unit	Total
...	...	...	...	...	...	...
...	...	...	...	...	...	...
...	...	...	...	...	...	...
...	...	...	...	...	...	...
...	...	...	...	...	...	...
...	...	...	...	...	...	...
...	...	...	...	...	...	...
...	...	...	...	...	...	...

TOTAL

Order date:

Delivery date:

CONDITIONS AND CLAUSES:

result in the garments not appearing in a store window and ending up in a corner because the principal spaces have already been filled. In the worst case scenario, it can be a reason for the client to return the collection.

With the emergence of the new system of constant updating of collections by large distribution chains, the multi-brand business now requires more renovation of garments in order to be equally competitive. This trend is reinforced by the increase in the sales area of stores, in detriment to the area devoted to warehousing, thus avoiding a build-up in stocks. Stores not only require the main collection of the season and intermediate orders to help sell it, but also tend to demand small segmented deliveries since they lack the storage space. The norm is to work only with the collection in the store, which demands promptness in deliveries and constant contact with the point of sale for possible repositioning.

DELIVERY CALENDAR

Spring-Summer	Month		Fall-Winter	Month
Precollection	January		Precollection	July
Main collection	February		Main collectionl	August
Christmas *flash*	April		Christmas *flash*	October

The prêt-à-porter calendar, with its two traditional spring-summer (delivered beginning in January) and fall-winter (beginning in June) seasons, is expanded with precollections (a month before the above-mentioned seasons) and seasonal updates (throughout the season itself).

Precollections

These are usually a continuation of the most-sold garments from the previous season, although they are becoming increasingly important in their own right and beginning to be independent. Their objective is not so much image or trend, but to provide a service to the store and contribute to boosting sales early in the season. Their price tends to be competitive, since they are offered during sales periods along with discount garments.

Flash sales and updates

Flash sales serve to cover concrete periods such as Christmas and New Year's, when party dresses are placed on sale, or summer, when bathing suits and accessories for the beach go on sale. Although the role of updates is to replenish the most-sold garments and update, as the name suggests, the main collection with designs not previously anticipated and that are now trendy.

POST-SALES SERVICE AND PENALIZATIONS

When the sale has been made, a relationship between designer-brand and store begins that does not simply end when the delivery of the order has been made. Post-sales service, of increasing importance, consists in minding delivery times, replacing merchandise during seasons, substituting defective garments, and supporting the brand in the store with elements of communication such as promotions and/or fashion shows.

This service is not only necessary for maintaining and reinforcing the relationship with the store, but also is essential in regard to the public. The repositioning of the clothes most in demand, changes, and solutions to possible problems have as their end consolidating the connection with consumers.

To make perfectly clear the limits of the relationship established with the point of sale, some stores, as a mode of protection, include penalization clauses in contracts in case some aspect of the negotiated services is not fulfilled. Retailers tend to be very demanding with delivery dates, to the extent that some may even end up penalizing the designer with charges or cancelling the order altogether. The first kind of penalization is serious since the more charges means the less the profit margins. But the second is even more grave as it entails the return of the entire order, with the consequent difficulty of replacement and the likely loss of a client.

There also are stores that stipulate profit guarantees in the contract, which means if they do not sell a certain percentage of the collection—quite high, between 60 percent and 70 percent—a penalty charge will be exacted on the designer, who, in this case, finds herself in a dilemma: rejecting the charge means losing a client while accepting it entails assuming the risk. It is advisable to accept the charge, under the condition that the merchant promises to make purchases during a certain number of seasons. In this way, one assumes the risk of being penalized and earning less if expectations are not met, but point-of-sale continuity is guaranteed for the mid-term.

Once the sales are secured, two parallel processes begin: production of the collection and conception and design of the collection for the upcoming season. Before this last process, it is advisable to reflect on how sales went and to what degree the collection was a success. In addition, it is a good idea to evaluate and assess criticism and other impressions received, all with the aim of determining if one is moving in the right direction, whether modifications are necessary, how to improve, and what needs to be made stronger. For this, sales figures are not enough, and the comments of clients are essential. This information will ultimately come in the form of returns, stocks, and complaints.

DISTRIBUTION

The objective of designers and brands, the same as anybody who introduces a product into the market, is to reach the consumer. Having a superb collection with the best fabrics, impeccable tailoring, and an unbeatable

Levi's Engineered Jeans wall bay

quality-price ratio is of little use if the collection never makes it out of the warehouse. Fashion has a very short shelf life.

Nowadays, the store is the place where designers and brands concentrate all their sales strategies, as it represents the initial contact with the consumer; for this reason it is imperative to control positioning from the start. It is not enough to place the collection in the establishment and sell it; one must convince consumers to return and buy again. As a result big-name brands go out of their way to control distribution to stores, genuine temples in which the goal is not merely making sales but converting the consumer

into an adherent of the brand. Spaces are conceived and designed to provide the visitor with an experience. They are places that seduce and excite, and where one's guide books recommend visiting—places that tell stories. The consumer is interested in a store where she feels comfortable, that is, one that meets her expectations, both emotionally and in terms of service. In this light, distribution has become essential to the definition of the identity of a brand.

A term much in use today in distribution is "concept store": stores that are a brand in themselves and whose strategy is conceived with this in mind. A product that wants to

become a brand requires advertising and other methods of communication, because on its own it says very little. Today, the consumer does not purchase the value of the product but the symbolic and added value it possesses. The store, as a space that envelops whomever steps inside, can utilize multiple elements to explain to the consumer what it is, harmonize with him, excite him, gain his loyalty.

The point of sale is thus a starting point for establishing a long-term relationship with the consumer. Occasionally, the main priority is not even to encourage instantaneous sales or impulse buys but simply to surprise. If buying has become a recreation, this idea goes a step further, making it a source of sensations and experiences. It is necessary at all times to know in what direction the distribution market is going. A beginning designer or brand must know not only where she needs to be, but also how to be there. Introducing a name in the market is expensive and requires time, but if one is in the right place, it is only necessary to attract attention to the product being offered. The consumer knows what he is seeing because he understands the context in which he is seeing it. It is for this reason that for an obscure brand, the only thing that can help to define its universe and communicate an idea of what it is, is the store. Being in one place or

© Nikita Ne4L Joukovsky. Traffic boutique

the other is definitive; and being there in one way or the other is, too. For all of the above reasons, it is important to choose a point of sale that is coherent with the style of the collection and where the garments will be able to make an impact. Over time, coherence generates solid brand identity; thus, it should be reflected in each and every collection, in the designs, in communication, and also in distribution. It is what gives the collection credibility in the eyes of the market and, consequently, creates customer loyalty.

There are various types of stores, differentiating themselves from each other according to the nature and variety of the products they sell, size, and/or the kind of public they are aiming at. Below, we take a look at each one individually.

THE MULTI-BRAND STORE

This is the traditional store that works more or less with brands according to their specialization. Normally, it covers only one sector (men's, women's, children's) and one type of product, for example, garments, undergarments, swimsuits, complements, etc.

Due to the emergence of large department stores and the success, for years now, of mass distribution and low-cost fashion chains, these stores have had to revise their thinking in order to stay afloat.

The new strategies are based on reducing the number of collections, taking special care in the selection process. This way the multi-brand store is able to specialize, though not by sector or product but rather by style, relying on secure values and recognized brands that guarantee high margins.

THE SINGLE-BRAND STORE

This is a store where we find the collections and garments of only one designer or brand. They can be upscale houses of great renown—Gucci, Louis Vuitton, and Prada—or large distribution chains—Gap, H&M, and Zara. In these stores, found in the main commercial and tourist centers of cities, everything down to the last millimeter is strategically employed to transmit the store's values.

Designers or brands that open a new business and opt for a single-brand store usually have only one branch, and thus total coverage of one's intended public is not guaranteed. For this reason it is ideal to expand and ultimately become a chain. One way of doing this is through a franchise shop, which consists in finding someone with a building or space who wants to open a store with a certain brand. It is the most economi-cal option, avoiding investment costs in real estate and management of the point of sale, although one of its drawbacks is that it prevents direct control of marketing.

LARGE DEPARTMENT STORES

These are large stores, aimed at a varied public, that offer a wide selection of brands and that may have their own brands. In this kind of business, normally collections are distributed by area, according to product type.

For a designer or brand just getting started, big department stores are a good way to emerge from obscurity because they draw in a lot of people, although given that they work with many different brands and in large volumes, the conditions they offer during negotiation are tougher.

Some brands, in order to stand out inside large department stores, enter with a corner or a shop-in-shop (a store within a store) whose main difference from a normal store has to do with size. A corner occupies a very small space; it may consist of a single exhibitor or be shared among several exhibitors. A shop-in-shop is larger and represents only one brand, but is responsible for furnishings, decorating the space and, at

© Daniel Grund. Levi's Flagship store in Berlin

Elche El Corte Inglés & Hipercor Shopping Center

times, providing a sales clerk. These methods offer the opportunity of creating one's own space inside large department stores and presenting oneself to the consumer directly.

OUTLETS

This is the channel for getting rid of stocks from previous seasons. The outlet can be a store that distributes several brands—a multi-brand store— or a single-brand establishment, in which case it tends to take more care in the presentation of the product.

SUPERMARKETS AND HYPERMARKETS

These usually have their own collections, although sometimes they carry brands directed at the general public, with aggressive pricing policies and discounts. Today, supermarkets that want to reach a public with more purchasing power are including high-end products in their general offer.

CATALOG SALES

The potential client first receives a catalog at home in which the products appear, with specific sizes, colors, and prices. Once the order has been placed, the purchase is sent to

Camilla Morais
TOP MODEL

Venca
Primavera Verano 09
Vívela!
www.venca.es
807 11 77 11

© Venca

the buyer's house, thus eliminating the need to actually visit the store. In this way, the demands of consumers who live in areas at a distance from big cities are met, which is one of the main advantages of this kind of purchase. From the first moment that the Internet appeared, brands that sell by catalog staked a claim on the 'Net, gaining not only the loyalty of their habitual consumers but also accessing new ones.

STREET MARKETS
Until recently they were the outlets par excellence, since it was here where stocks were sold. Now, however, they

are devoting themselves more and more to the sale of generic Asian products, at very low prices, that have no other channel of distribution.

THE WEBSITE
A website can serve as an additional tool of communication but also a marketing and sales platform, the business volume of which multiplies each year, thus becoming a useful way to begin to sell and enter into direct contact with the consumer. This phenomenon has altered the debate about the future of distribution: if until only recently it concerned choosing between a multi-brand or a

Ross + Bute website by Form Studio. Project management & art direction: Paula Benson; design: Paula Benson and Claire Warner

single-brand store, the debate now has begun to look at whether or not points of sale should be physical or virtual. If one chooses to distribute via online stores, the formula is almost identical to that of a multi-brand client, since it is the same type of business, only virtual. For the moment, though, the 'Net is mainly considered a point of support for conventional distribution.

Brands know that consumers today look for information about what they want on the Internet, go to the store to check the size and see how the garment looks on them, and compare prices between the physical establishment and the Internet, tending toward the one that is the most competitive. For now, the sales formulas that function best on the Internet are:
- Outlets (or special sales), which offer clothes that are out of season from major brands at half, or even a third, their original price.
- Virtual stores of luxury brands, which have sought recourse on the Internet primarily to stop the sale of copies and fraudulent items bearing their names online.
- Brands that offer personalization, giving the consumer the opportunity to create her own design, whether it be a garment, a sports shoe, or an accessory.

Selling over the Internet can help to sell the collection, but above all it is useful for unloading stocks and selling items where size does not present a problem and contribute to strengthening the brand, such as complements and accessories. If one begins to sell directly over the Internet it is necessary to control the information that appears on the website and manage stocks: one needs to be sure that all the products for sale online are in fact available. Also, it is important to indicate in a clear manner the payment method and the shipping time, as well as a telephone contact number in order to be able to resolve any problems that may arise, and prevent possible returns.

GLOSSARY

Branch: subsidiary retail house that belongs to an established store and is managed by it, generally smaller than the main store.

Brand identity: the assets and liabilities linked to the name and symbols of a brand, which add or take away value from it.

Catalog of references: work pages that contain a detailed description of each garment in the collection.

Chain: group of establishments belonging to a single company or that operates under the same management.

Client portfolio: brands and designers with whom a sales agent has contact, thus facilitating the negotiation of a possible sale.

Concept store: store that presents itself as a brand in itself due to its spectacular nature.

Corner: limited space inside a large department store, occupied by one or several brands.

Customer loyalty: the permanent loyalty of a specific public to a concrete product or brand, continuous or periodical.

Flash: small collections that serve to cover specific periods such as Christmas or New Year's.

Franchise: opening of a store of a particular brand by someone outside of the brand.

Large department store: large stores that offer a wide range of brands and products, and may, in addition, have their own brand.

Lookbook: a book that gathers all the garments that make up a collection.

Multi-brand store: store that contains the products of various brands, generally from a single fashion sector.

Order form: a document that details the amount of each design to be bought, as well as the specifications of the purchase.

Outlet: channel used to get rid of stocks from previous seasons.

Penalization: punishment or sanction applied as the result of a failure to comply with a regulation or agreement.

Post-sales service: service offered by a designer to a store where his or her collection is being sold, consisting of complying with delivery times, repositioning items during seasons, replacing defective garments, and supporting the brand with elements of communication.

Precollection: intermediary collection that joins the winter collection to the spring collection, and the summer collection to the fall collection.

Retailer: merchant that sells retail.

Sales agent: also sales representative, the professional in charge of introducing the collection of a brand or designer at a point of sale.

Sales representative: *see* sales agent.

Seasonal updates: repositioning of the most-sold garments of a collection and inclusion of unplanned designs that have become trendy.

Shop-in-shop: space inside a large department store occupied by a single brand, with the aim of presenting itself to the consumer directly.

Showroom: space where the clothes of one or more designers are exhibited, with the aim of selling them to stores.

Single-brand store: store that sells the collections and items of a single designer or brand.

Stock: amount of merchandise available for future use.

COMMUNICATION

Elements graphic design and art direction by StudioThomson, book image © Tim Bret-Day

COMMUNICATION

FASHION AND COMMUNICATION

Fashion is an act of communication in itself, a form of nonverbal exchange through which individuals express their identity and social belonging. In addition, fashion must communicate in order to sell, employing the right language for a product that changes rapidly every season.

Fashion is a unique system both for the way it functions—through always changing trends, ephemeral by definition—and for its market, which consists of big companies, luxury brands, and large-scale distribution.

Since dressing is a basic necessity, fashion has a very strong potential market and therefore its offerings must respond to a multi-faceted demand—all ages, both sexes, all social categories, and professionals.

The strength of fashion resides in the fact that it involves a market that is conducive to buying: styles are renewed each season and clothes deteriorate, making the potential sales of the sector infinite. Moreover, it is a market that knows perfectly well how to create necessity, generate demand, and provoke buying. Thus, exceeding mere usefulness and comfort, fashion has imposed a new logic: that of the power of seduction, which justifies the act of buying beyond the reasonable.

Fashion is legitimized through a socially disseminated media discourse whose main characteristic is communication. Its message is simple—trends—and is circulated visually in a spectacularly effective way—through advertising, fashion shows, brand image—adaptable to all media.

Today, communication is the indispensable focal point for managing any fashion brand. The product, advertising campaigns, fashion shows, boutiques, in short, everything that emanates from the brand and is related to it, emit messages that must be coherent with each other in order to communicate a strong brand image, always carefully maintained.

BRAND

Agents
- Directors of communication
- Branding agencies
- Marketing agencies
- Consulters
- Photographers
- Stylists
- Modeling agencies
- Illustrators
- Art directors
- Celebrity agents
- Others

Advertising agency	Media planning agency		Media
			- Press
			- Television
			- Radio
			- Internet
			- Point of sale
			- Others
Press agency, public relations and events			

Sector professionals
Trendsetters
End consumer

It is for this reason that today one of the main activities of a fashion company is production of this type of image, created with intangible elements of a symbolic and aspirational nature that are synthesized in visual messages such as photography, videos, fashion shows, collection of samples, etc.

PROCESSES AND AGENTS

Communicating fashion is normally a question of internal management where the designer ultimately assumes the role of the "great communicator." Decisions about the images to be used in a campaign, advertisement, website, etc. must ensure total coherency between the product and the images to achieve what one wishes to convey. The designer herself is her best means of promotion since, as a rule, she ends up becoming the visible representative of the values that the brand supposedly embodies.

But not all processes can be managed internally, and it is for this reason that

certain external agents are required for carrying out this work. They are professionals of a very heterogeneous nature including press offices, communications and public relations agencies, advertising and media planning agencies, modeling agencies, art directors and popular personalities.

THE PRESS OFFICE

This press team can be either internal or external to the company. Generally, the press office consists of a director (the press chief) and assistants responsible for writing communiqués and interacting with journalists to ensure that press releases are published. For this reason, it is extremely important that the press office be familiar with the professionals of different media so as to be able to identify their work, making working with a constantly updated database indispensable. This necessary degree of closeness and contact with journalists is the reason why press agencies always operate within the national sphere; if an agency is international, it

Anne Valérie Hash at French *Elle* March 2009

Anne Valérie Hash at Spanish *Vogue* March 2009

will have headquarters in the different countries where it operates.

One of the most important functions of the press office is to transmit a message that is coherent with the identity of the brand, something which requires total assimilation of the brand's culture and concept. There are many different ways to present this message to the media, which will subsequently disseminate it among the public. The most common is the communiqué. This is a precise text about a news item or a specific event structured in the following way: statement, a brief summary of the news that grabs the audience attention; body, the nucleus of the text that contains all the vital information that one wishes to transmit; and the ending.

Through clippings, a collection of all the appearances of the brand or designer in the media in the form of news, the press office can evaluate its work, both quantitatively (the number of publications in which the communiqué has appeared) and qualitatively (the number of media outlets that have spoken positively about the brand), and extrapolate information.

PUBLIC RELATIONS
The aim of public relations is to promote the image of the brand among

Vincent Schoepfer
Paris

Automne Hiver 09/10 collection little house

Pour l'HIVER 09, Vincent Schoepfer s'inspire de la célèbre série américaine, que nous avons toutes et tous adoré, « la petite maison dans la prairie » - une collection ludique, colorée tout en poésie.

Ce jeune créateur franco-suisse revisite les incontournables, comme la veste smoking revue et corrigée façon cuir, ou la chemise à carreaux détournée d'un plastron gris.
Le plastron « must have » de la collection cette saison, joue la couleur, en flanelle ou en coton. Amovible, il habille aussi bien les chemises smoking que les polos à manches longues.
Le liberty, toujours d'actualité, se porte sous des pulls en maille ajourée rouge, gris ou noir.
Pièce phare de la saison, le pantalon carotte habille toutes les silhouettes, quelles soient sobres ou décalées, décontractées ou plus classiques.

Enfin, plusieurs pièces de ses précédentes collections sont repensées ou revisitées, comme le « sweat » aux épaules colorées ornées d'un passepoil fluo, la ceinture de smoking en forme de gilet, ou, la veste de costume avec ceinture intégrée.

Diplômé d'ESMOD, Vincent Schoepfer, jeune créateur français, confirme ainsi sa 6ème collection. Passionné par les couleurs et les matières, elles restent un vaste espace de jeux et de création illimitée.

Vincent Schoepfer est distribué dans des multimarques « créateurs » en France et à l'international.

Liste des points de vente : www.vschoepfer.com

This winter 09, Vincent Schoepfer gets inspiration from the famous tv show that we all used to watched « Litlle house on the Prairie », a playful, colored collection in poetry. This Young French-Swiss designor revisits the inescapable, as the dinner jacket in leather or the squarred shirt diverted with a grey plastron.

The plastron is a real must have this season. Its plays with colors and fabrics. Removable, it dresses as well elegants shirts as the long-sleeved polos.
The liberty, still trendy, goes under grey or black, red openwork pullovers in stitch. Key piece of the season, the carrots pants dress all the silhouettes, which are sober , relaxed or more classic.
Finally, several pieces of Vincent Schopefer 's previous collections are rethought or revisited, as the sweat with colored shoulders , the belt of dinner-jacket in the form of vest, or, the jacket of suit with integrated belt.

Awarded by ESMOD, Vincent Schoepfer, young creator, so confirms his 6th collection. Fascinated by colors and materials, they remain a vast area of games and unlimited creation. Vincent Schoepfer is distributed in multibrands "creators" in France and on the international stage.
List of the selling points: www.vschoepfer.com

Contact presse - POULAIN&PROUST
Ouarda Coussay - Marie Aude Poulain
131 rue saint denis 75 001 paris
tel +33 1 55 80 75 14 - fax + 33 1 55 80 75 15
ouarda@poulainproust.com

Poulain & Proust Communication for Vincent Schoepfer

STEPS IN THE DESIGN OF AN ADVERTISING CAMPAIGN

Advertising objectives

Briefing

Focus of the campaign

Basic message of the campaign

Media plan

Budget

Proposals

Presentation to client

Implementation of the campaign

end consumers and especially sector professionals and trendsetters that talk about the brand to the media and, in turn, provoke media to talk about the brand.

Managing the public relations of a brand involves controlling all its external manifestations, including presentation of the collection of samples, launching a new line, fashion shows, opening a new store, special events (society affairs, benefits, sponsorships, etc.), endorsements in the form of lending or giving garments to celebrity personalities, and management of VIP relations.

As all of this supposes a delicate and complicated activity. It is advisable that the person devoted to public

relations be involved in the structural organization of the brand.

THE ADVERTISING AGENCY

A brand or designer looks to an advertising agency when appearance in the press or on television via a publicity campaign becomes a necessity. Due to the high cost of campaigns, in the world of fashion only big-name brands use ad agencies, as smaller ones lack the necessary resources.

Companies can opt for a specific agency or hold a contest among several and then choose the proposal that best fits what they want to communicate.

The three main actors in an advertising agency are:

XXL brands in action for The Brandery

- The account executive: responsible for making a connection between the agency and the brand, and for bringing the process to a successful close while respecting established conditions and times.
- The creative director: develops the concept of the ad campaign.
- The art director: in charge of the aesthetic and visual components of the campaign, and translating and interpreting the philosophy of the brand through images.
- The copywriter: responsible for the written aspects of the campaign.

The first step in developing a campaign consists of a meeting between the agency and the client—the brand, usually represented by the designer, brand or product manager, and sales director—in which the latter conveys to the advertising executive the identity of the brand, the advertising goals, and the kind of public that the campaign is intended for. After this meeting the agency draws up a briefing, a document summarizing all the information that will serve as the basis for the campaign.

After the briefing, the account executive puts together a team to carry out a situational analysis in which positioning and profits of the brand are identified, in addition to performing market studies and searching for new ways to evaluate the relationship between the brand, the product, and consumers. All this information will determine the focus of the campaign, giving impetus to a creative

(continued on p. 158)

XXL brands in action for Custo Barcelona

The first Kate Moss for Topshop collection launches in the London flagship store

strategy. Along the lines of this plan, a basic message for the campaign emerges and the channels or means by which it will be distributed become clear, a step in the process normally delegated to an agency specialist: the media planner.

The creative part of the campaign follows. It is developed by the art and creative directors who, keeping in mind the budget they have to work with, come up with a series of proposals that are accepted, rejected, or modified. With the client's approval, the agency then develops the originals for print.

Once the campaign has been launched, the process is controlled and monitored in order to evaluate its success and impact on sales.

Since all campaigns involve a complex process and require that the agency embrace the culture and spirit of the brand, the best results are obtained by maintaining a prolonged relationship between the agency and the client.

CELEBRITIES
Because of their lifestyles and high visibility in today's entertainment culture, celebrities of film, music, sports, and society celebrities, have become

Respect Me by Missy Elliott for adidas Originals

ideal trendsetters in the realms of fashion and style. The media grants them wide coverage, and consequently potential consumers aspire to identify themselves with the brand that the celebrities represent.

Fashion companies, for their part, look to celebrities for advertising campaigns, for being present as spectators at certain events such as fashion shows or the inauguration of stores, for promoting their products on special occasions (for example, giving them designs to wear at the Academy Awards) or for developing advertising through product placement.

Product placement

This is the predominate trend in communication today. Brands appear in movies or on television, which is an efficient way to present a product to someone and see how well it sits with them. Garments have a context; they are placed in a false-real paradigm created so that spectators will want to buy them.

When product placement is done in films, given that the production process is long, what one tries to sell is not a product but rather the image of the brand. The intention is to establish a connection between the char-

acter and the brand, which normally is only done with positive figures, generating a big emotional charge such as the case of the recently graduated journalist who enters unexpectedly into the world of fashion in the movie *The Devil Wears Prada*. Some film directors closely connected to brands and this type of advertising are Pedro Almodóvar and Sofia Coppola.

When this technique is applied to television, placement is carried out in series, with presenters, in music videos, commercials, or through appearances by leaders of public opinion. The time that elapses between the shooting of the promotion and its broadcast is short, and thus the intention here is to sell products; what the presenter is wearing today can be bought in stores tomorrow. The television series that has had the most success in this respect is *Sex and the City*, where the personalities of the characters are identified with brands, for example, Carrie with her Manolos.

INSTRUMENTS OF COMMUNICATION

A series of elements allow for a dialogue between the brand and the consumer—the so-called "instruments of communication." These instruments can be divided into two types: institutional instruments of communication, used to transmit the values of the brand, and temporal instruments of communication, the aim of which is to promote the product.

INSTRUMENTS OF INSTITUTIONAL COMMUNICATION
The brand
More than a name or a logo, a brand is the story that one wishes to tell, the objective of which is to stimulate desire in the consumer. It communicates the mission and vision of the company regarding desired positioning through coherent and permanent communication, recognized beyond the mutability of the products.

It is increasingly difficult for brands or fashion designers to distinguish themselves from peers, as products tend to be similar in price and quality. It is for this reason that branding has become such an important instrument: it tells stories about the brand that help stimulate desire and emotions among consumers, primary motors of consumption in society today. In other words, it represents the power of the brand as an element of differentiation.

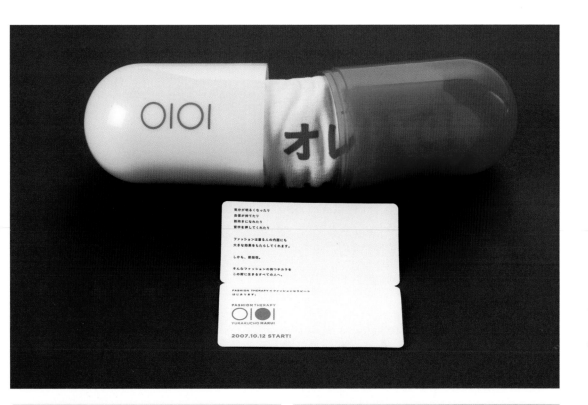

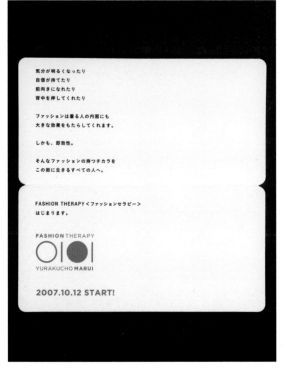

Branding is a part of the species of marketing that was born in the mid-eighties, when brands began to assume the central importance that they enjoy today. As a result, advertising does not announce the simple existence of products but must create an image and tell a story about a brand. As the French semiologist Roland Barthes stated in *The Fashion System* (1967), "It is not the object but the name that creates desire."

Every brand comes into being with the desire to triumph and gain recognition. It should not be forgotten that fashion, above all, is a business. Moreover, in today's so-called "liquid society," analyzed by sociologist Zygmunt Bauman in *Liquid Life* (2005), brands have become the access points to our identity. Their objective is to establish connections between individuals in order to create a brand community, gathered around certain aesthetic values, preferences, and specific tastes, thus creating a cultural idea or certain identity toward which they aspire. As individuals, our primary desire is to be recognized as part of a community. It is for this reason that humans imitate, though not randomly; they always choose their models. When buying they define themselves through their relationship with the objects and the meaning society attributes to them (the materialization of values that the brand provides) and as such, with the purchase of certain products, one will feel part of the community created by the brand.

100 % COTTON

WASH INSIDE OUT
WITH SIMILAR
COLORS
RESHAPE AND
STRETCH INTO
SHAPE IMMEDIA-
TELY AFTER GENTLE
WASH WHILE
GARMENT IS STILL
MOIST
BY IRONING THE
MOIST GARMENT
YOU CAN RETAIN ITS
ORIGINAL SHAPE
SOME SHRINKAGE
MAY OCCUR

36

IVANAhelsinki+

Homemade in Finland
Did you know that you
can also take care of your
clothes by airing, brushing
and storing them well

38

IVANAhelsinki+

Homemade in Finland
Did you know that you
can also take care of your
clothes by airing, brushing
and storing them well

Branding includes elements that help in the overall construction of the brand. These are divided into tangible and intangible characteristics:

- Tangibles: the graphic identity or image of the brand, such as the logo, name, color, slogan, or packaging.
- Intangibles: the personality or idea of the brand, consisting of values, promises, cultural references, stories, myths, etc.

Labels

These are one of the tangible elements of the brand that offer the most information about the designer and the product. Some indicate the name of the designer or brand and explain the characteristics of the fabric and how to care for it, as well as the "made in" information. As for the first type of labels, it is necessary to pay attention to the design because in a boutique along with other garments it will represent the first contact with the buyer. In fact, not only are they important because of the technical information they offer to the consumer, but also because of the need to care for the image of the brand. These labels can change their design each season, reflecting the spirit of the collection.

The second group of labels ensures that the consumer can take care of the garments properly as the provider customarily includes directions about how to care for the fabric with specific symbols. Included are the place of

Puma at Volvo ocean race. © Sally Collison

manufacturing and a reference to the manufacturer or designer, someone to contact in case there is a problem.

Point of sale

Nowadays this space is of capital importance within the sphere of communication, as it is the meeting point between the brand and end consumer. It is the place where the strategy of the brand takes physical shape, creating and transmitting the desired atmosphere so that the client can have the kind of buying experience that makes him willing to pay a surcharge. It is for this reason that single-brand stores are increasingly more important from a strategic point

of view, some having become genuine brand temples (for example, Prada with its "Epicenters") where what matters is not so much selling but generating an experience intricate to the idea of the brand as a lifestyle.

Patronage and sponsorship

The relationship between fashion and other sectors often materializes in these two forms. A brand utilizes patronage—providing financial support to others so that they can do their work, without asking for anything in exchange—to improve its image, becoming involved in an activity of general interest and making clear its commitment to social participation,

Puma @ Volvo ocean race. © Sally Collison

as Prada does with its Foundation and Benetton with Factory. With sponsorship a brand provides a loan, essentially economic, to a team, individual, program, or communication medium for advertising purposes. It should be noted that this is not a disinterested loan, because the entity or person being sponsored will be held to certain obligations to the benefactor, such as wearing the logo of the brand in a visible way.

Art and music are two of the most common sectors used by brands for communicating in this form, always when the figure being sponsored has already achieved prominence in the public's mind.

Corporate magazines

These are less common communication tools used mostly by large consumer brands to create customer loyalty and are distributed in their stores, as is the case with H&M. They include information and images from the collection as well as news and reports related to the brand or the world of fashion in general.

The website

Today the Internet is an indispensable tool for communication. It is the way to introduce oneself to the world, not just to clients but anyone interested in a brand or designer. The website should be true to the image of the brand and constitute a perfect instrument for deepening advertising discourse and creating interactivity, offering the possibility of entering into direct communication with the brand. It is important to remember that the clients of a designer can come in two forms: the retailer and the end consumer. Both are interested in image and in seeing the collection, though the former is more concerned with obtaining information about the professional trajectory of the designer and mode of contact, while the latter wants primarily to know where to buy the collection. Despite this, many brands still use the website only as a showcase for reproducing the images of campaigns and/or collections and not for generating an exchange of information with consumers and potential clients. This is because two of the most important aspects of having a website are making sure the content is specific to the online medium—that is, it should be conceived with the Internet in mind— and be updated continually.

SEASONAL INSTRUMENTS OF COMMUNICATION

These instruments are devoted exclusively to promoting the product, and involve elements that have a short duration and whose appearance and content vary with each season.

The lookbook

The lookbook consists of a series of images from the collection whose objective is to transmit the image of the brand and evidence to the public that identifies emotionally with the company. Thus, the garments are shown by models or at least atmospherically (for this reason a clothing stylist in charge of looks and props, when these are used, takes part) and are delivered to clients, buyers and stylists.

The catalog

The catalog is one of the most traditional avenues of communications for showing the collection in the world of fashion, although today, especially thanks to the Internet, it has lost some of its importance, being replaced by different digital supports. In contrast to the lookbook, it is done with flatter photographs as opposed to production images, offering more information and characteristics about the product.

The press dossier

Generally, it is a CD destined for the press that contains a series of images (high resolution for printing and low resolution for posting online) and accompanying text in different languages. The text consists of a brief commercial description, written in

paragraphs, that can be read together or separate. Due to these characteristics, it is a tool utilized very often when composing notes, writing reports, or making reference to a brand.

Fashion shows

These are the medial jewels of communication in fashion. By nature they effectively combine business practices with the art of entertainment. The deep interest of the media in fashion models, celebrities, and star designers gives fashion shows undeniable appeal. While fashion shows began as a simple means of presenting collections to clients, nowadays they are a great tool for communication, capable of producing a visual declaration of the principles of a brand.

The wide coverage granted to fashion shows by the media in the form of television reports, magazines, newspapers, and on the Internet has replaced a strictly professional public—professional buyers, journalists, and private clients in the case of haute couture—with a global consumer who, fascinated by the pageant of glamour on fashion runways, has become the reason for this mode of promotion.

Design: Luxoir. SS 2008, *MIRAGE* at Pasarela Cibeles Show

© Dan Lecca. Anne Valérie Hash's AW 2008-2009 ready to wear show

Given the tremendous media display involved and the resources they consume, questioning the actual necessity of fashion shows is not unwarranted. Is such excess truly necessary? Are so many famous faces needed in the front rows? Must one have a fashion show in order to survive in the world of fashion? Still, it must not be forgotten that the primary objective of a fashion show is to sell. And what better platform for this than an authentic media show, a unique spectacle broadcast to and for a global audience.

The fashion show has the advantage of showing products through direct presentation, which allows the audience to react to the latest styles instantaneously, thus contributing to a sense of privilege among the attending public of knowing beforehand the latest trends in the world of fashion.

The process of planning and presenting a fashion show demands knowledge of the organizational steps needed for making it a success. The investment in material and human resources is high, and thus it is extremely important to obtain an attractive return,

(continued on p. 174)

FASHION WEEKS CALENDAR

	Fall-Winter					Spring-Summer						
Women	January	February	March	April	May	June	July	August	September	October	November	December
	Berlin, São Paulo, Hong Kong	New York, London, Milan, Madrid, Copenhaguen	Paris, Los Angeles, Tokyo			São Paulo	Berlin, Hong Kong	Copenhaguen	New York, London, Milan, Madrid, Tokyo	Paris, Los Angeles		
Men	January	February	March	April	May	June	July	August	September	October	November	December
	Milan, Paris, Berlin, São Paulo, Hong Kong	New York, London, Madrid, Copenhaguen	Los Angeles, Tokyo			Milan, Paris, São Paulo	Berlin, Hong Kong	Copenhaguen	New York, London, Madrid, Tokyo	Los Angeles		
Haute Couture	January	February	March	April	May	June	July	August	September	October	November	December
	Paris						Paris					

whether in the form of sales or media impact. It is for this reason that the fashion show must be coherent with the spirit and image of the brand, taking into consideration all the elements that contribute to best comprehending the collection.

One of the first planning decisions that needs to be made is deciding in what international context the brand will be situated, as the prêt-à-porter fashion weeks have particular characteristics, ones that can have either a positive or negative impact on the perception of a designer.

The prêt-à-porter fashion-show calendar is very compressed, and it is

© Dan Lecca. Walter Van Beirendonck, SS 2009, *eXplicit* collection

difficult to obtain a slot on days with as many as twenty shows. As a result, great effort is expended each year on obtaining a spot.

The presentation of women's fashion lasts for two months: February and March for fall-winter collections and September and October for spring-summer collections beginning in New York and then followed by London, Milan, and Paris. Meanwhile, men's prêt-à-porter collections appear in January and July in Paris and Milan, immediately after the haute-couture fashion shows. In addition to these "official" fashion weeks, many others are cel-

ebrated in countries such as Spain, Brazil, Japan, Australia, Portugal, India, and Russia, which each year contest for a place on the calendar and have the capacity to attract buyers and gain press in the international sphere.

In addition to deciding where the collection will be shown, it is important to be aware that there are different kinds of fashion shows that can help define the brand being presented:
- The classic fashion show usually has a spatial arrangement consisting of a central catwalk, with the audience on both sides, and photographers and a backstage at both extremes.

(continued on p. 178)

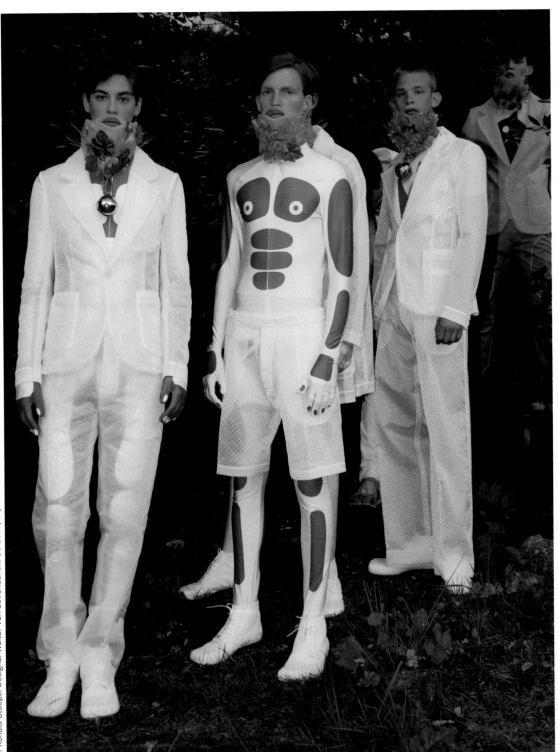

These shows are usually presented by brands with a "genetic code," such as Giorgio Armani, Prada, and Ralph Lauren, which reassert their position season after season.

- The entertainment fashion show allows for better representation of the product thanks to a more "showy" production. Big-name brands in the luxury market, such as Dior or Chanel, with the resources and the desire for maximum visibility for their collections normally opt for this type of show.

- The conceptual fashion show is more reserved and concentrated. Its main focus is the message of the collection, transmitted with maximum efficiency and a minimum of resources. It is often the choice of designers interested in a production format much removed from the glamour of entertainment fashion shows, as is the case of Belgian designers Martin Margiela and Walter Van Beirendonck or Japanese designer Rei Kawakubo of Comme des Garcons.

Alternative modes of discourse to the fashion show exist, used by small brands interested in finding a niche for themselves within the fashion landscape. Used by the likes of Bruno Pieters, Marcel Marongui and Bern-hard Wilhelm, these can include presentations of collections at art galleries—digital or virtual—or executed via any support medium that permits the appropriate exhibition of a designer's work. Also important to keep in mind when conceiving a fashion show is proper development of the message of a collection in order to strengthen the key concepts one wants to transmit, adapting them to the language they require and the audience they are intended for. Toward this end, in the planning stages of a fashion show, one of the most important steps is the formation of a team consisting of:

- The events or art director who decides on the positioning, message, and language of the presentation, as well as handling coordination of different activities and teams.

- The production manager in charge of the location, stage management, music and lighting technical teams, security, backstage, and post-production.

- The stylist or product manager responsible for selecting and providing garments and complements.

- The casting director who selects the fashion models according to their type and the attitude they project.

- The director of communications responsible for communication planning, invitations, press releases and

© Carole Desheulles. Première Classe

press kits, seating (how to arrange the public in the front rows), media relations, and maintenance.

A fashion show supposes a significant investment in communication for a brand that must take into account factors such as proportion, impact, and returns. How the budget is allocated among production, casting, communication, protocol staff, hair dressing and makeup, stage manager stylist, prop manager, set designer, DJ, etc. should therefore always be kept in mind. For calculating the return, an evaluation system must be established in which each element needs to be reviewed: calendar placement, location, theme, audience, team, scenography, design, lighting, music, casting, and, of course, the collection. The evaluation process ranges from the amount of sales to buyers to media impact. The latter is measured not simply by the quality of media opinion about the fashion show but the length of the news item and the positioning of the designer within it.

All of these factors make the fashion show a strategic tool with a double impact: one, in the long term, through the establishment of the image of the brand and, the other, in the short term, as a point of reference in the construction of the commercial aspect of the collection. It is for this reason that a fashion show, as appealing as one may be, must be considered as a whole as a coherent strategy in the general context of a brand or designer.

M.C.B.

Fairs

Fairs or shows, discussed earlier, represent a meeting point between different actors in the sector, and for this reason they have become an instrument of communication for companies nowadays.

MEDIA

The media spreads information, opinions, and entertainment among a wide-ranging public. The indispensable source of financing for most of the media is investment in advertising. In the case of fashion, cosmetic and perfume brands invest the most in media, especially in the press.

THE PRESS

Accounting for the majority of advertising investment, the press is the most important medium of communication in the world of fashion. One of its great advantages is that it is a medium in which the advertiser—the brand—chooses the duration of the campaign as well as when it will take place, in addition to being a mode of communication that has a direct influence on the act of buying.

There are various types of press:

– Daily

– Periodical

– Specialty

The daily press

Fashion coverage in the daily press tends to be little, depending on the mastheads. Dailies include fashion in supplements or in their culture, society, and trend sections, and the majority of articles about fashion appear during fashion-show periods, with regular in-depth treatment being a rarity.

One of the daily papers with the most credibility in the world of fashion is the *International Herald Tribune*, with a section managed by Suzy Menkes, the guru of fashion journalism today.

As for advertising, dailies are advantageous given that they have a wide coverage, a delineated audience, and prestigious mastheads. Disadvantages include the excessive heterogeneity of their audience, and inferior graphic quality.

The periodical press

This consists of women's magazines divided among widely respected publications with international editions such as *Vogue, Marie Claire* and *Elle*, to name a few; magazines aimed at the general public such as *Citizen K* and *Glamour*; trendy publications such as *i-D, Purple,* and *Self Service*; and lifestyle magazines such as *Wallpaper** and *Surface*. Each magazine has a certain public in mind, prese-

lected according to its content, with the advantage of the use of color and superior graphic quality of images than the daily press.

Periodicals offer more fashion content and involve two kinds of specialized professionals:
- Stylists or fashion editors responsible for selecting garments from among different collections for each issue.
- Fashion journalists who write text for publications based on trends and images.

Brands especially invest in this type of press, and it has become a norm for the brand to appear in magazine pages in one form or the other. As such, companies influence the textual content of fashion magazines, and as a result the periodical press is being used more and more as a self-promotional campaign.

Women's press, especially the high-end variety, is the mode of communication preferred by fashion brands since the two have a relationship of reciprocal necessity: the need of the press to appear before readers as the arbiter of the companies that determine fashion and the need of brands to see their products and their universe appreciated by a potential client.

The masthead of the magazine confers a part of its own image to the advertiser. Therefore the impact of a brand will differ if it chooses a prestigious magazine, which offers its guarantee to the products it presents, as opposed to an image-generating magazine, which positions itself as an aesthetic trendsetter. In the same way, the image of a magazine is established in accordance with the brands it promotes.

The specialty press

This is the press concerned exclusively with the fashion industry and includes reports about fashion shows, news about designers and collections, and information concerning projects and innovations in the sector. The advantage of this type of press is that it examines its subject in depth. Its international reference is *Women's Wear Daily*, the first daily newspaper containing economic and financial information about the fashion industry, founded in 1919 by American Edmund W. Fairchild and considered today the bible of the profession.

TELEVISION AND RADIO

Television is a medium that exerts great social influence but is very expensive. The products it advertises are mainly perfumes and accessories, mostly for special dates such as Christmas, Mother's Day or Father's Day.

Television places attention on the transience of fashion and the sector's most spectacular facet: fashion shows and star designers. Beyond this, fashion coverage is almost absent on television. During fashion shows, news programs normally transmit the most spectacular images without much commentary, though these are not always the most representative of the spirit of the collection.

Some television segments are devoted to fashion, normally in the form of magazine TV, but most are defined by a society reporting style. As a reference, it is worth mentioning such programs on French television, a pioneer in devoting space to fashion, as *Dim Dam Dom* (1965), *Paris, c'est la mode!*, produced by France 3 and transmitted also by France 5, and *Paris Modes* of Paris Première. Noteworthy on American television are *Style with Elsa Klensch*, broadcast by CNN from 1980 to 2001, and the channel Fashion TV.

Radio is not an ideal medium for an essentially visual sector. While some programs examine the current state of fashion, radio is more often used to generate sales during specific dates such as Christmas.

EXTERIOR ADVERTISING

Particularly characteristic of an urban setting, this mode of communication is directed at a public on the move. It is an efficient and profitable medium—thousands of people can be reached at a low cost—and has a strong impact due to its great visibility and wide coverage. It consists essentially of billboards, luminous vertical panels on sidewalks, banners, illuminated signs, banderoles, and placements on public transport. This method of communication, which started out being used by big consumer brands, has become an ornament of urban architecture (especially for companies such as Calvin Klein, DKNY, and Armani).

The synergy between the press and exterior advertising allows for appropriate communication of the strategies of different product lines. Thus, while haute couture and prêt-à-porter construct an image in the press that consumers aspire to, accessories and perfumes guarantee the democratization of the brand through exterior advertising.

GLOSSARY

Aspirational: aiming at situating or positioning a person above his/her actual socio-economic or cultural level.

Branding: term used in marketing to designate the creation of an image or a story regarding a brand.

Briefing: document that summarizes the information upon which a campaign will be based, offering instructions for its development.

Carrie: main character in the series *Sex and the City*, played by Sarah Jessica Parker.

Celebrity: commonly known person with a high degree of media coverage and attention on the part of the public.

Clippings: collection of all the appearances in the form of news of a brand and/or designer in the media.

Copywriter: professional in charge of writing the texts for an advertising campaign.

Endorsement: lending or transfer of garments to celebrity personalities.

Instruments of communication: elements that allow for a dialogue between the brand and the consumer.

International Herald Tribune: daily publication with the most credibility in the fashion world.

Manolos: shoes by the brand Manolo Blahnik.

"Official" fashion weeks: shows held in New York, London, Milan and Paris.

Patronage: financial assistance given to a brand or others so that it can perform its work, without asking for anything in return.

Press dossier: CD directed at the press that contains a series of images and an accompanying text in different languages about the brand and/or its products.

Press office: team responsible for communication and interaction so that a brand appears in the media.

Press release: precise text concerning a news item or event.

Product placement: form of communication that consists in presenting a product within a context, whether through television or cinema.

Sidewalk panels: luminous vertical panels installed on sidewalks.

Sitting: distribution of the public in the first rows of a fashion show, the responsibility of the person in charge of communications.

Sponsorship: when a brand provides assistance—essentially economic—to a team, individual, program, or media for advertising purposes.

Trendsetter: opinion maker.

VIP: socially important person because of fame, power, or influence.

***Women's Wear Daily*:** first daily newspaper with economic and financial information about the fashion industry.

RECOMMENDED READING

Agins, T. *The End of Fashion. The Mass Marketing of the Clothing Business*. New York: Morrow, 1999.

Barthes, R. *El sistema de la moda*. Barcelona: Gustavo Gili, 1978.

Baudot, F. *Mode du siècle*. Paris: Éditions Assouline, 1999.

Boucher, F. *Histoire du Costume en? l'Occident de l'Antiquité à nos jours*. Paris: Flammarion, 1983.

Bravo, A. *Femenino singular: la belleza a través de la historia*. Madrid: Alianza Editorial, 1996.

Butazzi, G. *La Mode. Art, Histoire & Societé*. Paris: Hachette, 1983.

Chenoune, F. *Des modes et des hommes. Deux siècles d'élégance masculine*. Paris: Flammarion, 1993.

Corbellini, E. and Saviolo, S. *L'esperienza del lusso. Mondi, mercati, marchi*. Milan: Etas, 2007.

Davis Burns, L. and Bryant, N. *The Business of Fashion: Designing, Manufacturing, and Marketing*. New York: Fairchild Books & Visuals, 2002.

Deslandres, Y. *Le costume, image de l'homme*. Paris: Éditions Albin Michel, 1976.

Dickerson, Kitty G. and Jarnow, J. *Inside the Fashion Business*. New York: Prentice Hall, 2002.

Drumbach, D. *Histoires de la mode*. Paris: Regard, 2008.

Erner, G. *Victimes de la mode. Comment on la crée, pouquoi on la suit*. Paris: Éditions La Découverte, 2004.

Evans, C. *Fashion at the Edge*. New York: Yale University Press, 2003.

Everett, J. and Swanson, K. *Guide to Producing a Fashion Show*. New York: Fairchild, 2004.

Gehlhar, M. *The Fashion Designer Survival Guide*. New York: Dearborntrade Publishing, 2005.

Jernigan, M. H. and Easterling, C. R. *Fashion Merchandising and Marketing*. New York: Prentice Hall, 1997.

Johnson, M. J. and Moore, E. C. *Apparel Product Development*. New York: Prentice Hall, 2000.

König, R. *Die Mode im Zivilisationsproze?*. Munich-Vienna: Carl hanser Verlag, 1985.

Lipovetsky, G. *L'Empire de l'éphemère. La mode et son destin dans les sociétés modernes*. Paris: Éditions Gallimard, 1987.

Lurie, A. *El lenguaje de la moda*. Barcelona: Paidós Contextos, 1994.

Martin, R. and Koda, H. *Haute Couture*. New York: The Metropolitan Museum of Art, 1995.

Monneyron, F. *La mode et ses enjeux*. Paris: Klincksieck, 2005.

Nieder, A. and Heimann, J. (ed.). *20th Century Fashion 100 Years of Apparel Ads*. Cologne: Taschen, 2009.

Olmo Arriaga, J. *Marketing de la moda*. Madrid: Ediciones Internacionales Universitarias, 2005.

Ormen-Corpet, C. *Modes XIXe-XXe siècles*. Paris: Hazan, 2000.

Remaury, B. (dir.). *Dictionaire de la Mode au XXe siècle*. Paris: Éditions du Regard, 1994.

Richou, S. and Lombard, M. *Le luxe dans tous ses états*. Paris: Economica, 1999.

Salgado, J. and Blanco, X. *Amancio Ortega, de 0 a Zara*. Madrid: La Esfera de los Libros, 2004.

Saviolo, S. and Testa, S. *Le imprese del sistema moda. Il management al servicio della creatività*. Milan: Etas, 2000.

Sicard, M. C. *Luxe, mensonges & marketing. Mais que font les marques de luxe?* Paris: Pearson Education Frances, 2003.

Silverstein, M. J. and Fiske, N. *Trading up. The New American Luxury*. London: Portfolio, 2003.

Stephens Frings, G. *Fashion From Concept to Consumer*. New York: Prentice Hall, 2004.

Stone, E. *The Dynamics of Fashion*. New York: Fairchild, 2004.

Tellier-Loumagne, F. *The Art of Knitting*. London: Thames & Hudson, 2005.

The Kyoto Costume Institute (ed.). *Fashion. From the 18th to the 20th Century*. Cologne: Taschen, 2005.

Tungate, M. *Fashion Brands. Branding Style from Armani to Zara*. London: Kogan Page, 2005.

VV. AA. *Lèche-vitrines. Le merchandaising visuel dans la mode*. Paris: IFM-Regard, 2003.

Wadell, G. *How Fashion Works Couture, Ready-to-Wear and Mass Production*. Oxford: Blackwell Science, 2004.

Wells, K. *Fabric Dyeing and Printing*. London: Conran Octopus, 1997.

DIRECTORY OF FASHION DESIGN SCHOOLS

AFRICA

TUNISIA
ESMOD Sousse
Angle Av. Mohamed Maarouf
Tahar Sfar
Sousse
www.esmod.com.tn

ESMOD Tunis
33 bis, Av. Charles Nicolle
1082 Tunis
www.esmod.com.tn

AMERICA

BRAZIL
IED São Paulo
Rua Maranhao, 617
São Paulo
www.ied.it/Network/San-Paolo

Senac São Paulo
Avenida Engenheiro Eusebio
Stevaux, 823
04696-000 São Paulo
www.sp.senac.br

UNITED STATES
Fashion Institute of
Technology
7th Avenue 27th Street
New York, NY 10001-5992
www.fitnyc.edu

Parsons The New School for
Design
560 7th Avenue
New York, NY 10011
www.parsons.edu

Pratt Institute
200 Willoughby Avenue
Brooklyn, NY 11205
www.pratt.edu

ASIA

CHINA
ESMOD Beijing
Nº 1, 34 Dongsanhuanzhonglu
District Chaoyang
1000020 Beijing
www.esmodbeijing.com

INDONESIA
ESMOD Jakarta
JL Asem Dua Nj3-5
Cipete – Jakarta Selatan
12140 Jakarta
www.esmodjakarta.com

JAPAN
Bunka Fashion College
3-22-1 Yoyogi – Shibuya-ku
Tokyo 151-8522
www.bunka-fc.ac.jp

ESMOD Osaka
1-21-25 Kitahonie
Nishi-Ku
Osaka
www.esmodjapon.co.jp

ESMOD Tokyo
3-29-6 Ebisu
Shibuya Ku
Tokyo 150-0013
www.esmodjapon.co.jp

Joshibi University of Art
and Design
1-49-8 Wada
Suginami
Tokyo 166-8538
www.joshibi.ac.jp

Kobe Design University
8-1-1 Gakuennishi-machi
Nishiku
Kobe 651-2196
www.kobe-du.ac.jp

Mode Gakuen
Nagoya Mode Gakuen
4-25-13 Meieki
Nakamura-ku
Nagoya 450-0002
www.mode.ac.jp

Osaka Mode Gakuen
3-3-2 Umeda
Kita-ku
Osaka 530-0001
www.mode.ac.jp

Sugino Gakuen
4-6-19 Kamiosaki
Shinagawa-ku
Tokyo 141-8651
www.sugino.ac.jp

Tokyo Mode Gakuen
1-6-2 Nishi-shinjyuku
Shinjyuku-ku
Tokyo 160-0023
www.mode.ac.jp

Vantan Design Institute Osaka
2-8-5 Nishi-Shinsaibashi
Chuoh-ku, Osaka-shi
Osaka 542-0086
www.vantan.com

Vantan Design Institute Tokyo
1-9-14 Ebisu-minami
Shibuya-ku
Tokyo 150-0022
www.vantan.com

LEBANON
YWCA
Rue Houston Bacha
Ain EL Mraisseh
BP11 2041 Beirut
www.esmodbeyrouth.com

SOUTH KOREA
ESMOD Seoul
528-8,9 Shinsa Dong
Kangnam Ku
Seoul
www.esmod.co.kr

SYRIA
ESMOD Damas
Bab Moussalla immeuble
A–Awkaf
4ème étage
Damascus
www.esmod-syrie.com

UNITED ARAB EMIRATES
French Fashion University
Esmod Int'l Dubai
Academic City – Block 4
Al Ruwaayah
Dubai
www.french-fashion-university.com

EUROPE

BELGIUM
Artesis Hogeschool Antwerp –
Fashion Department
Nationalestraat, 28/3
2000 Antwerp
www.antwerp-fashion.be

Flanders Fashion Institute
Nationalestraat, 28/2
2000 Antwerp
www.ffi.be

La Cambre
21 Abbaye de La Cambre
1000 Brussels
www.lacambre.be

FRANCE
Atelier Chardon Savard
15 rue Gambey
75011 Paris
www.acs-paris.com

École Duperré
11 rue Dupetit-Thouars
75003 Paris
www.duperre.org

ESMOD
16 Boulevard Montmatre
75009 Paris
www.esmod.com

ESMOD Bordeaux
11 cours Edouard Vaillant
33000 Bordeaux
www.esmod.com

ESMOD Lyon
87 rue de Sèze
69006 Lyon
www.esmod.com

ESMOD Rennes
6 place des Colombes
35000 Rennes
www.esmod.com

ESMOD Roubaix
27 Bvd. du Général Leclerc
59100 Roubaix
www.esmod.com

Institute Français
de la Mode
33 rue Jean Goujon
75008 Paris
www.ifm-paris.com

Istituto Marangoni
12 avenue Raymond Poincaré
75116 Paris
www.istitutomarangoni.com

Parsons Paris School
of Art and Design
14 rue Letellier
75015 Paris
www.parsons-paris.com

Studio Berçot
29 rue des Petites Ecuries
75010 Paris
www.studio-bercot.com

GERMANY
ESMOD Berlin
Görlitzer Strasse, 51
10997 Berlin
www.esmod.de

ESMOD Munich
Fraunhofer Strasse, 23H
80469 Munich
www.esmod.de

THE NETHERLANDS
ArtEZ
Onderlangs, 9
6812 CE Arnhem
www.artez.nl

Gerrit Rietveld Academie
Frederik Roeskestraat, 96
1076 ED Amsterdam
www.gerritrietveldacademie.nl

Hogeschool voor
de Kunsten Utrecht
Ina. Boudier-Bakkerlaan, 50
3582 VA Utrecht
www.hku.nl

ITALY
Accademia di Costume
e di Moda
Via della Rondinella, 2
00186 Rome
www.accademiacostumeemoda.it

Domus Academy
Via G.Watt, 27
21040 Milan
www.domusacademy.it

IED Milano
Via Pompeo Leoni, 3
20141 Milan
www.ied.it/Network/Milano

IED Roma
Via Branca, 122
00153 Rome
www.ied.it/Network/Roma

IED Torino
Via San Quintino, 39
10121 Turin
www.ied.it/Network/Torino

IED Venezia
Isola della Certosa
30141 Venice
www.ied.it/Network/Venezia

Istituto Marangoni
Via Verri, 4
20121 Milan
www.istitutomarangoni.com

Polimoda
Via Pisana, 77
50143 Florence
www.polimoda.com

NORWAY
ESMOD Oslo
Sandakerveien, 76 A
0484 Oslo
www.esmod.no

SPAIN
BAU, Escola Superior
de Disseny
Pujades, 118
08005 Barcelona
www.baued.es

Escuela Internacional
de Diseño y Moda ISA
Andrés Mellado, 6
28015 Madrid
www.academiasisa.com

Escuela Superior de Diseño y
Moda Felicidad Duce
Guillem Tell, 47
08006 Barcelona
www.fdmoda.com

ESDi
Marquès de Comillas, 81-83
08202 Sabadell, Barcelona
www.esdi.es

IDEP
Gran Vía, 461
08015 Barcelona
www.idep.es

IED-Istituto Europeo di Design
IED Barcelona
Torrent de l'Olla, 208
08012 Barcelona
www.ied.es

IED Madrid
Flor Alta, 8
28004 Madrid
www.ied.es

UNITED KINGDOM
Central Saint Martins College
of Art and Design School of
Fashion and Textiles
107-109 Charing Cross Road
London WC2
www.csm.arts.ac.uk

Edinburgh College of Art
Lauriston Place
Edinburgh EH3 9DF
www.eca.ac.uk

Istituto Marangoni
30 Fashion Street
London E1 6PX
www.istitutomarangoni.com

Kingston University – Faculty of
Art, Design and Architecture
Campus Knights Park
Kingston upon Thames
Surrey KT1 2QJ
www.kingston.ac.uk

London College of Fashion
20 John Princes Street
London W1M 0BJ
www.fashion.arts.ac.uk

Manchester Metropolitan
University – Faculty of Art
and Design
Campus All Saints, Edificio
Chatham
Cavendish Street
Manchester M15 6BR
www.artdes.mmu.ac.uk

Middlesex University – School
of Arts and Education
Campus Cat Hill
Barnet EN4 8HT
www.mdx.ac.uk

Newcastle University – School
of Arts and Cultures
The Quadrangle
Newcastle upon Tyne NE1 7RU
www.ncl.ac.uk

Royal College of Art – School of
Fashion and Textiles
Kensington Gore
London SW7 2EU
www.rca.ac.uk

University of Brighton – Faculty
of Arts and Architecture
Grand Parade
Brighton BN2 0JY
www.brighton.ac.uk

OCEANIA

AUSTRALIA
ESMOD Australia
2 Short Street
Sidney NSW 2010
www.esmod.com.au